Relationship status

My survival guide to love, dating and heartbreak

Anastasia Kingsnorth

EBURY
SPOTLIGHT

1 3 5 7 9 10 8 6 4 2

Ebury Spotlight, an imprint of Ebury Publishing
20 Vauxhall Bridge Road
London SW1V 2SA

Ebury Spotlight is part of the Penguin Random House group of companies
whose addresses can be found at global.penguinrandomhouse.com

Copyright © Anastasia Kingsnorth 2024

Anastasia Kingsnorth has asserted her right to be identified as the author of this
Work in accordance with the Copyright, Designs and Patents Act 1988

First published by Ebury Spotlight in 2024

www.penguin.co.uk

A CIP catalogue record for this book is available from the British Library

ISBN 9781529929461

Typeset in 12/20pt Adobe Caslon Pro by Jouve (UK), Milton Keynes
Printed and bound in Great Britain by Clays Ltd, Elcograf S.p.A.

The authorised representative in the EEA is Penguin Random House Ireland,
Morrison Chambers, 32 Nassau Street, Dublin D02 YH68

 Penguin Random House is committed to a sustainable future for our business, our readers and our planet. This book is made from Forest Stewardship Council® certified paper.

For my beautiful mother, this one is for you.

Contents

Introduction xi

Chapter 1 **1** **Hook Ups and Online Dating**
   6   Online vs offline – how do I meet people?
   15 Let's set up my online dating profile
   33 Holiday flings

Chapter 2 **39** **The First Date**
   47 How do I make the first move?
   52 Where should we go for our first date?
   54 Dating is different depending on where you live
   64 What do we talk about?
   71 The double date

Chapter 3 **81** **Red Flags and Warning Signs**
   86   Horror dating stories
   90   Ghosting
   93   Toxic behaviour
   94   The overlap
   109 Setting boundaries
   112 The dreaded ick

Chapter 4 **123** **Being Single**

130 It all begins within

134 The pressure from society

138 Valentine's Day

Chapter 5 **153** **Entering into a Relationship**

158 Dating with an online presence

167 The soft launch

172 Let's meet the family

178 Meeting friends

182 What do I wear?

184 He hasn't introduced me to his friends... what does it mean?

185 What if I don't get on with his family and friends?

Chapter 6 **187** **Relationships that Go the Distance**

196 Situationships

199 Open relationships

204 Friends with benefits

207 Keeping it in the friendship...

216 How do I know if I have found my soul mate?

219 Signs you're in a healthy relationship

Chapter 7 225 **The Breakup**
226 Knowing when to let go
229 Handling the breakup
233 Relationship breakup vs situationship breakup
237 Closure
244 Getting under to get over . . .
247 Moving forward and setting boundaries
249 The exes
257 How would a new partner take you being friends with your ex?

Chapter 8 261 **Lessons I Have Learnt**
262 How you love yourself is how they will love YOU
267 How did I learn to love myself?
274 Choosing myself

Acknowledgements   282

Glossary   287

Introduction

IF YOU ARE trying to date in the twenty-first century, you are most definitely going to need a guide, or a map, or both. Since when did something that should be so easy become insanely difficult?

Dating comes with its challenges. Forty years ago, if you had asked your partner what a red flag was, they would have said a flag that is red, not a relationship turn-off. If you asked them what the ick was, they would probably ask if that was even a real word. Either dating has got harder or we have over-complicated it to the point that it is now serving impossible.

Hello, my name is Anastasia, and I am trying to date in my twenties. If you don't know who I am, I am a 23-year-old woman living in Manchester and I have shared my life online with my generation for the last 12 years. Whilst I have been growing up on a screen in front of many of you for my entire teenage life, I have done one hell of a lot of growing up behind the screen too. I have experienced my fair share of horrendous dating stories and found myself in some questionable but hilarious situations, like the time when I was dating a boy and he went missing for five minutes because he was upstairs sleeping with his ex. Or the time I thought blind dates were a good idea, but after finding someone I liked and him spending a few months getting to know me, he decided to date one of my friends. Oh, or the time I got hit by a car on a first date. You're about to hear it ALL, so I hope you have a drink at the ready. Now, for the first time, I am excited to share with you everything I have learnt about men, dating and myself in this almost-guidebook to dating and navigating our lives in our twenties. You will also hear from two of my best friends – Saffron, on long-distance relationships and her take on dating in the public eye, and Byron, on dating in the gay world and all the tea on the situation we found ourselves in a few years ago . . .

There's a reason behind every heartbreak and this is my reason. When I first started writing this book, I had recently come out of my first real relationship, through no wrongdoing on the part of either of us, but purely because I felt like I needed to be single and begin my self-love and growth journey to discover what I truly wanted from dating. It allowed me to spend time alone, reflect on past situations and dates and discover what the dating world is like in the current climate. I want to take you along with me on the journey of beginning my dating life again, from setting up my dating profile, DM slides I have received, recent first dates and hook ups, as well as a deep dive into my dating past purely for your entertainment.

This book is a journey of my emotions, relationships and real-life stories that I never thought I would have the guts to share. I unpack some extremely heavy topics; dissect why I have been in so many failed situations and delve into the world of online dating to try to understand it. There is a lot of pressure at my age to find your forever person and be building a life with someone in that relationship, but this book isn't about that. It's filled with tips and tricks to help you based on what I have learnt, but more than that, it is a celebration of being single, and a guide on how to love yourself through it all. This book is real, it's raw, and it has taught me the true meaning of dating, and who the real person I should be dating right now is.

I want you to read and enjoy this book whether you are currently in a relationship or single. You don't have to be on a solo self-growth journey to take something from this read, you just must be open-minded to bettering the current version of yourself to maintain a current relationship or be ready for one when it approaches you. Or be happily single for the rest of your life – it's whatever the hell you want it to be.

This is modern-day dating, and how the f*** to get around it, so let's dive right in.

Chapter 1

Hook Ups and Online Dating

WE'RE GOING STRAIGHT into the nitty gritty – the hook-up stage. This is something I haven't had to worry about for nearly a year now, but as I have recently become single again, I'm starting this book at the very beginning.

Oh, the joys of hook ups. I have a love/hate relationship with this aspect of dating; in some ways I find it exciting – getting to meet new people, not having to worry about what anyone else is thinking, just being carefree and enjoying myself. On the other hand, I find it quite draining; being back at square one, faced with the challenge of finding someone amongst the male species all over again, occasionally experiencing self-doubt and questioning my worth, and dealing with a lot of the crap that men love to throw our way. Doesn't that sound appealing?

So, what exactly counts as a 'hook up'? I honestly think that anything from a kiss all the way to sealing the deal could sit comfortably under this term. One-night stands could potentially fit here too, but that is a bit of a grey area. I would only call it 'hooking up' if you're doing it more than once, whereas a one-night stand is quite literally what it means – you only do it once.

I've experienced several versions of a hook up in my time, most of which tend to happen on party holidays abroad when, to put it politely, you turn into a feral version of yourself with no care in the world. One of my favourite memories was while I was in Australia, backpacking. We were on the last leg of the trip in Cairns and this was actually our final night out in Australia, so we wanted to make it as memorable as possible. I was dared to go up to a random boy and simply say 'shut up and kiss me' in the hopes that he would, in fact, shut up and kiss me. To my surprise, it worked; he stayed silent and kissed me, and apparently liked it. So much so that he followed me around for the rest of the evening hoping we'd have a one-night stand. However, sadly for him it didn't make it quite that far. Maybe he liked my confidence, or maybe he was just drunk. Either way, it's a great hook-up story. To make the story even funnier, the next day we were flying home and we had just got to the airport to check our cases in, and he was also there, checking his cases in. I honestly thought, *Surely not*. Out of the thousands of boys I could have picked to kiss the night before, how have I picked one that is in the same place as me the next day? We arrived at our boarding gate and saw him sat there, and we all just started silently laughing. We couldn't quite believe it, it was really one of those 'wow the world is very small' moments. What would have topped it off was if I had to sit next to him on the flight home, but thankfully this was not the case!

If we are talking going further than just a kiss, I have a few stories in that department too. As we are discussing Australia, we'll keep the stories to this trip. I did a three-day boat tour around the Whitsunday Islands. Firstly, it was incredible, and I would highly recommend it – not just for the views of the clearest water and beaches I have ever laid my eyes on, but also for the views of the incredible staff on board, who were hired in no small part because they were good-looking! When we got on board, I straight away set my sights on one boy in particular. He was the chef, so was it the fact that he was good-looking or that he could cook? I'll let you decide. The kicker was that the first words he spoke were to tell me that he was good friends with a boy who broke my heart when I was younger, and he had seen me on his socials before. So now, was I getting with him because he was good-looking, a chef, or to annoy the boy I was heartbroken over? I can confirm it was option one with a hint of option two – I'm not that shallow!

As the days on the boat went on, I started to fancy him more and more. He was the quiet one out of all the boys on the ship, but in a way that intrigued me. I think I enjoyed the mystery of it, as I couldn't work out if he also fancied me. On the second night, I ended up speaking to him for a lengthy amount of time, long enough for my friends to wonder what on earth we were talking about. They started to record me so I had it on film forever, just in case we ended up together in ten years and wanted to look back on our first conversation. (Spoiler: that sadly is not the case.) I came back to my friends and explained that once we left the boat the following day, the crew would go to an after party in the local town, and they had asked us to join. Internally I was screaming, but externally I kept my cool.

I had not used makeup or done my hair for the whole time we were travelling, so this was an excuse to bring out the makeup and hair straighteners and get glam. We got all ready, went to meet them, and had the best evening. I may have got slightly tipsy and ended up back at his house. On the way in, I had to walk past his house mate and introduce myself. This is where I died inside. I'm not ashamed to admit I started to feel a little embarrassed about what I was doing. The friend definitely must have thought, *Oh, here comes another girl*. I think I can spare the details of what happened next, but yes, we had a little fun before I went back to the hotel. Rating my experience overall, it was exciting, a fun holiday story to tell and I thoroughly enjoyed my three days. What I didn't enjoy as much was the raging UTI I was gifted as a farewell present – thank the lord for cranberry juice!

Online vs offline – how do I meet people?

I think meeting new people is actually very hard these days, particularly in person because I never know what someone's intentions are, whereas online, depending on the dating app, you can get a slightly clearer reading of what the other person is looking for because they will write it on their profile for people to see. Judging by my past experiences, apart from holiday flings, a good 80 per cent of boys that I have been with, I have met online on a dating app. Even though this has been the case thus far, I would love to just randomly bump into someone in the street, look straight into their eyes and fall madly in love, because what a story that is to tell. Sadly, the chances of this happening are not in my favour. Even meeting someone in a bar, or through a friend – just in a more natural environment – sounds so much more exciting than having to set up another online dating profile.

As fun as that sounds, I just don't think that's going to happen for me. Meeting people online is all I have ever really known, so I think setting up my dating profile would probably be the best option at the moment for me to dip my toe back into the dating world. But which dating app should I use? Don't worry, I have tested the waters on pretty much all of them, so you don't have to.

HINGE

This is a personal favourite of mine, as I think the men on there put more effort into their profile. You have the option for six-plus photos, and three prompts to help the person looking at your profile get to know you a little better. They have even recently introduced the voice prompt, where you can speak about whatever you want about yourself, or you can get your friend to describe you, which is always a little fun one to come across amongst thousands of similar profiles. A favourite prompt of mine is the two truths and one lie option, as I think that's a nice way to start a conversation when messaging someone.

TINDER

I'm not a fan of this one. I think it requires minimum effort to set up a profile, and it's more photo-based than personality-based, as it's a simple swipe left or right. Let's be honest, this is probably 90 per cent based on the way you look, rather than the one sentence you can write that appears at the very bottom of the screen of the person who is scrolling. I also think this one is used for more of a hook-up, one-night-stand scenario, but maybe I just haven't personally heard any Tinder success stories.

RAYA

This one is a little different as far as dating apps go because you actually have to apply to be on it and wait to get accepted. I applied over four years ago and only got accepted last year, so it took me three years to see what the hype was all about. When you hear people talk about this app, the word celebrity is probably what you associate it with. There are SO many celebrities on it, but also just regular people with a highly paid job. You know everyone is 100 per cent real on it, as they have had to link their Instagram to verify it's them. The only annoying things are a) the price – it is over £100 a year and I honestly don't understand why, and b) you only get to swipe a certain amount of people a day. I understand this because there aren't that many people on the app, so if you continuously swiped for hours, eventually after a few days you may have swiped everyone. But the people the app shows me often live somewhere else in the world, so it makes the likelihood of something actually working out very slim. I have also found that people are just not as chatty or forward on there. Maybe they think they are too good for dating apps, or maybe they got it for the same reason as me, just to be nosey about who was on it. You can't screenshot on the app, otherwise you get kicked off, and you're not allowed to publicly reveal who you've seen on there, but let's just say I have come across some very famous people . . .

BUMBLE

This one is a little different as the boy cannot message you first; instead, you message them. I haven't really used this one too much, as it slightly scares me because I want the man to message me first so I know he is interested, but maybe I should give it a go.

The next one is an app I don't have much personal experience with, so I'm handing over to an expert here to take you through this one . . .

Grindr?

Grindr? G-R-I-N-D-R? You're probably reading and re-reading that and assuming you're seeing things, but no, I can confirm we are about to talk about Grindr. Not a salt grinder, nor a grinder you would you use to crush meat. Well, maybe there are some similarities with that one. The INFORMASS gay dating app... ahhh, right yeah. This is the part where I should probably tell you it's no longer Anna writing this. Unless of course you want to imagine Anna cosplaying as a gay man looking for 'love' on a dating app that is flooded with unsolicited dick pics and a multitude of horny gay men, then be my guest. No kink-shaming here.

It's Byron (Anna's friend) and, yes, I have partaken in sex with men *crowd gasps* and apparently I am the best person in Anna's life to speak to the gays on a level only a gay man could. I don't think we need to dive too deeply into my love life and who I have and haven't had sex with... [*that's for my own book jk*] but yes, I have indeed downloaded Grindr a few times... then deleted it... then downloaded it again... then deleted it – and the cycle continues. Or at least it did for that period of my life.

Firstly, if you're looking to find love on Grindr you're looking in the wrong place. Unlike Tinder,

Hinge and all the rest of them, people on Grindr very much skip the small talk and the getting to know you. In fact, that's a lie, they'll often ask if you enjoy being penetrated or being the penetrator. How romantic! I mean, that's great if you're looking for a one-night stand, but it doesn't often result in the most romantic situations.

So, here's my guide to Grindr – for heteros . . . !

You've downloaded the app, decided whether you want to put a picture of yourself on there, added a few interests and a little bit about you – don't get this mixed up with other dating apps, this isn't where you're going to start giving your life story or thinking of quirky prompts.

Horny gay men want one thing and one thing only, and that's why creating a profile and giving it some personality isn't important. In fact, you could probably find sex on there without even showing your face. I can almost hear the disappointed tuts coming from all the mums' mouths, *Is this really what the world has come to? Everything revolves around sex!* Now, Karen, let's not pretend you haven't read *Fifty Shades of Grey* front to back four times over, and not because you like the storyline or the character development, you horny bugger!

In a nutshell, Grindr allows you to see gay people in your area with the ability to chat to them and potentially arrange to meet up and recreate a scene from *Fifty Shades* – just less vagina and not catered to the gaze of middle-aged women.

Like I said, I've dabbled in Grindr. I've had hook ups with strangers and exchanged passionate messages with someone ten metres away that could potentially be my neighbour. I've been 'lucky in love' throughout my time on the app and I've not had many horror stories from my endeavours, but I have found myself in a few awkward situations.

For example, 'Omg, are you Anastasia's friend?', 'I think I've seen you on YouTube before', 'Aren't you the guy that did that annoying ad about uni that is always on my TikTok?' Yes, these are all correct, but I think the story that takes the cake is finding out that the stranger I just had sex with had followed me online and watched my YouTube videos for years but failed to mention that beforehand. Although, on reflection, I'm grateful he didn't say anything because that might've been a little awkward.

Okay, let me set the scene ... Second year at uni, my flatmates are out, I'm horny and suddenly online looking for sex. (Sorry, Mum!) There's a knock at my door and it isn't the Amazon driver delivering my parcel, it's actually the man I just arranged to come over ten minutes prior, delivering his penis. (The delivery time is a lot quicker than Amazon actually; maybe they should start hiring horny gay men to deliver their parcels.) I shall skip the details of what happened next and just let you know that I took the precaution of hiding anything of value, or anything that suggested I had a career on the internet, as you would when inviting a complete stranger into the safety of your own home. Oh and also avoiding the awkward conversation of 'Are you a porn star or do you make YouTube videos, because the eight tripods and three cameras around your bed are really throwing me off here?' Anyway, we have sex. I walk him to the door and see him on his way. The end ... Only I wish that is how our interaction had ended ... In fact, this is how my time on Grindr ended. This was the nail in the coffin, the thing that made me delete the app for good. (Well, until I decided to stalk my now ex-boyfriend on there, to try to make him fall in love with me – but that story is for another time. Spoiler alert: it worked!) The man who I'd just been naked with decided to turn around to me as I waved him off and say, 'Congratulations on hitting 100,000 subscribers, by the way.' In that moment, my proudly just-used penis shrivelled up inside me and I wanted to combust into a tiny million pieces.

So, yes, using Grindr to have sex with strangers might seem fun but proceed with caution because you could find yourself in a very embarrassing situation or, even worse, meeting a murderer. I'm still figuring out which in that moment I would've preferred.

Seriously, though, if you're a gay man exploring your sexuality and you decide to download Grindr, please be extremely careful. If you're going to go round to a stranger's house or if you are inviting them to yours, let a friend know as a just in case – it's always better to be safe. There are a lot of horrible people out there and you could very quickly and easily find yourself in a dangerous situation. Go touch yourself or something instead.

Let's set up my online dating profile

I have decided after trying the majority of the dating apps that I am going to go back to my old faithful, Hinge. I feel comfortable on this app as this is where I have found success before, so I hope I find it again. For me, having just come out of a relationship, it just feels like a familiar place to start and I'm feeling surprisingly excited about making a whole new dating profile and all the new people I am going to come across.

When it comes to setting up a dating profile, the best place to start is the prompts. This is the stage where you've filled in all of the basic information that everyone has to fill in and you finally get to make your profile your own and a touch more personal. On Hinge, there are so many to choose from:

- My most irrational fear.
- Together, we could ...
- Two truths and one lie.
- A fact about me that surprises people.
- Dating me is like ...
- This year I really want to ...
- Typical Sunday.
- Give me travel tips for ...

I like these as it's a little insight into you as a person, but if you're clever enough with your answers, you can receive some great responses and see the person's sense of humour. Setting up my profile, I am going to use:

- This year I really want to ... *get off Hinge*
- Give me travel tips for ... *exploring your home town*
- Dating me is like ... *waking up and realising you have another two hours until your alarm*

- Two truths and one lie ... *I can hold my breath underwater for four minutes, I have skydived from 15,000 feet over Australia and I've broken both of my arms*

I don't want to spoil any of the fun, so I will let you figure out which one is the lie!

Or another option is to theme your responses. This can be a nice way to make someone laugh and get them to slide into your messages. For example, I know someone who is competitive, so they based their profile on always having to win ...

- Typical Sunday ... *is me winning at Monopoly*
- My most irrational fear ... *is losing*
- A fact about me that surprises people is ... *I never lose*

In my time on Hinge, I have seen several profiles set up like this, and I think it shows a sense of humour. Looking at the responses that one of my friends gets to her profile, which has a similar set-up, it's a winner. The likes are flooding in, and instead of just liking a photo, she is getting actual responses that she can reply to, sparking a good conversation with someone – as opposed to them calling you pretty or complimenting you and it never developing any further. However, despite her success here, I think I'm going to stick to my varied answers. This way, the conversations that men will attempt to start with me should hopefully all be different, yet still witty and humorous.

Now, when it comes to which pictures to choose, this is a whole other ballgame. Even though I think the prompts are technically more important, let's be honest with ourselves, a good percentage of men flicking through our profiles are first seeing your photo, and will only continue to scroll down if they find you remotely attractive, as sad as that is.

I have seen several different photo options on Hinge. Do you use a selfie? Do you use a photo where you're all glammed up? Do you use a more natural, laughing photo rather than one that is so posed? Or do you use a group photo? I personally like to use a more natural photo for the first option, and avoid the group photo until photo four or later, as they may think you are one of your friends, or fancy of your friends more, which we want to avoid. A classic male response. To top off the photo section, if you have a dog, use that dog like you have never used it before. As a dog lover myself, when I see a dog appear on a man's profile, I'm already envisioning our whole life together, children, marriage, the full thing. A pet is always a winner on a dating profile and a dog walk could even be cute for a first date if you prefer to meet during the day.

With six photos and three prompts, your dating profile is pretty much complete. You have given the right amount away for someone to want to start a conversation with you, but you have left them wanting more. Now you're ready for responses.

THE RESPONSES

The responses, despite your profile being top tier, are always going to be questionable. But this is where the fun begins – choosing which cheesy chat-up lines to respond to and which to leave where they belong: in your requests. This time on Hinge, even though it has been a very short period of time, I have received a fair few interesting responses. These are a few of my favourites.

In response to the *Two truths and one lie*:
- I hope they are all true, I don't want a liar
- You deffo can't hold your breath underwater
- You cannot hold your breath for four minutes, behave
- You look like Jason Momoa, so I believe the underwater one
- Broken arms is cap
- The breathing one, that's too impressive

In response to the *This year I really want to get off Hinge*:
- I have a plan to get us both off it
- Want a reason to get off it then?
- Odds on we both delete it
- I'll delete it off your phone on our first date
- Now we've found each other, we don't need it
- Why are you even on here?

In response to the *Give me travel tips for exploring your home town*:
- My parents' house
- I know a nice alley we could take a visit to
- Now you're someone I want to take home
- I know the best place for a bottle of wine
- Home is where the heart is, after all
- To be fair, there is a huge 24-hour Tesco we could get snacks from

Finally, the responses to my photos ...
- Ngl I wish I was your bed so bad
- You can have my children
- I need a wife as hot as you
- You're a gift from the gods
- Yeah, our kids would be models

After reading those responses, I'm sure your faith in humanity and love is restored because the romance is bursting through the pages ... No, you probably lost a few brain cells, if we're being honest.

What makes it worse is that these responses are from men on Hinge, which I claim is the best dating app. However, within the many bad ones there are a few good ones I could respond to. I think I will avoid the one who claims I look like Jason Momoa, though – he has such a way with words I would never know how to respond to him.

When replying to messages on dating apps, I always like to go for something witty, or if I am the one sliding into their messages first, I prefer getting a prompt. If I am being completely honest, I don't think I am the greatest at sending messages first. A lot of my friends constantly slate me for using the super-cringey line of 'hey you' to slide in with, and I can't even blame them for the slander, it is cringe. It does, however, work. I have used this several times and I'm not sure if the reason I get a response is because the line is so incredibly good, or because no one else was sliding in and I was the only option. Either way, it doesn't do much conversationally, but it is a last resort if you really cannot think of anything else.

My top ten ways to slide in would be . . .
1. Hey you (*This just has to be number one*)
2. You must be the guy who said we're going for a drink?
3. Where have you been all my life?
4. You look a lot like my future boyfriend
5. You look like you're going to ruin my life
6. Can I tell you I fancy you in person?
7. Your place or mine?
8. Titanic – sorry, that was a terrible ice breaker
9. You found me!
10. Fancy you

I don't like to go overly cringey with the chat-up lines, but I feel like these are the right level to entice the other person without embarrassing myself. But these chat-up lines don't just work for dating apps, I think a lot of these, if not most, are more suited to Instagram, which is arguably the biggest and best dating app of them all. I haven't ever met a partner through Instagram but I think it is very easy to do so, and I do know a few people who have.

INSTAGRAM

One of my best friends, Saffron, met one of her ex-boyfriends through Instagram, and her story will always be one of my favourites.

I was on Tinder – this was many years ago before I decided this app was not for me – and I came across a boy who happened to be a twin. Saffron and I have always said how amazing it would be to date best friends, or brothers, or even better twins, so when I saw he was a twin and they were both good-looking, I instantly had to tell her. I matched with one of them and got speaking for a while, then we took it over to Instagram DM and carried on getting to know each other there. It lasted a few weeks then fizzled out; it was during lockdown so we'd almost exhausted every conversation and I think we both just lost interest.

To both of our surprise, it went a little different for Saff. I found out his twin's Instagram and passed it onto her, and she fancied him so decided to follow him. One thing I love about her take on dating is she will NEVER message the man first. She firmly believes that if he wants her, he will put in the effort and message first. This is rubbing off on me and I much prefer this to sliding in first now. We were waiting a few days to see if he would message her or follow her back, which he did, and he replied to her story. They got chatting and eventually exchanged numbers, which led to several cute date nights on FaceTime until they could eventually meet once restrictions were lifted. This relationship then lasted for two years. It is crazy to think that if I hadn't downloaded Tinder and matched his twin, would their paths ever have crossed? I think this is an example of everything happens for a reason and what is meant for you simply will not pass you by.

Instagram is a great way to gain more insight into the person you want to speak to, as you can see all their photos; not just the best six on a dating profile, but also the dreaded tagged photos. Honestly, if you want to give yourself the ick over someone, go down their tagged photos. You are so welcome. Although sometimes the tagged photos can be a nice surprise, some people have them turned off, and that's when you know you should probably exit while you can. This could be a tell-tale sign that they're potentially a catfish and using someone else's photo to create a fake profile, or alternatively it could be a sign that they heavily edit their photos. I have experienced this in the past where someone messaged me hundreds of photos of himself that he had posted, but had his tags turned off. I thought something looked a little odd with his face in the photos because the lighting always lit up his face in exactly the same way, no matter what the photo, and this seemed like too much of a coincidence. After being the ultimate stalker girl I am, I managed to find a photo of what he actually looked like, which was completely different. I hate to admit it, but I do love a little stalk of someone's Instagram. Even if they don't have it linked on a dating app, I will always try to find it as I just think it's interesting to look at, and who doesn't love being nosey?

Diary Entry

While writing this chapter of the book, I experienced a slightly embarrassing moment on Hinge that part of me is kicking myself for, but then the other part of me is telling myself this happened for a reason. I was swiping, as you do, and I came across this boy — lovely profile, lovely pictures. His job intrigued me the most as he is a dermatologist, so I was like, wow, this boy seems cool. We matched and were speaking on Hinge all night. I hate even admitting this, but although my Hinge notifications were off, I was running to this app every ten minutes to see if this boy had replied. Something about him excited me so much, I don't even know why.

To my surprise, he asked if we could take it off Hinge, so we switched to message; I was up until 2am speaking to him and I went to bed feeling like a child on Christmas Eve. This is where it went slightly wrong. As girls do, we stalk — we love a good stalk of the profile — and I went on the tagged photos to see, you know, the real side of him. I started looking on his friends' profiles to find more photos of him and, yes, okay, I sound like an extreme stalker but don't act like we've not all been there. But then what did I do – I only went and accidently liked one of his friend's photos. The ground might as well have swallowed me up there and then. I immediately unliked it, and hoped his friend didn't see, but of course he did. Why does this this happen to me?

I've woken up this morning to this boy ignoring ALL of my previous messages, and instead he says I have liked his friend's Instagram photo and his friend claims we have also matched on Hinge and spoken. I can't lie, for about an hour I was gutted; I was also confused because I do not recognise the friend at all, so I'm going to assume we matched before I got with my ex-boyfriend, so we are talking minimum seven or eight months ago. But after an hour of feeling guilty for such a silly mistake, I realised that only a BOY reacts this way, and a man would see the bigger picture.

It's so funny because this situation has happened to Saffron and me in the past. I matched with this boy over a year ago, then a few months ago he matched with Saffron. When she showed me, I laughed and said, 'Oh my God, I've matched with him in the past, he is lovely, you should definitely speak to him!' That is the difference between how girls react and how boys react.

I looked at it from both sides, and if I had matched with his friend yesterday and was flirting with him all day, that is more than fair, and I would understand the bluntness I received. But the fact that it was over a year ago? No thank you, this situation was not a loss for me.

Being back on dating apps is an interesting one for me, especially after that experience, and I feel like I love them one day and other days I completely lose hope in them and feel like I'm going to be single forever. Saying that, I have decided to branch out from Hinge and re-download Bumble. Truthfully, this stemmed from the fact that I was lying in bed last night scrolling through Hinge for longer than I care to admit, and I was having no luck. Slightly embarrassing, and I felt almost deflated. Or maybe it's not embarrassing; I think it's normal to feel like there is no one out there for you. Of course, that is NOT true, and I reminded myself of that this morning and I already feel a lot better. I know I'm going to have those days and the most important thing to realise is it's okay and I should never feel guilty for feeling sad over it some of the time. Like I said, I did take the plunge and download Bumble again, and I must say I'm not hating it. I haven't found anyone that has caught my eye just yet but something about a new layout of a new app, new men and a new profile brought back that excitement about dating. I'm currently enjoying the fact that the girl must message first, but let's be real, the novelty of that is going to wear off in a few days and I'll be back on Hinge replying to another person guessing my two truths, one lie prompt.

ANNA X

THE DREADED DM SLIDE...

After speaking about sliding into people's DMs on my podcast (*Sex, Lies & DM Slides*) for the last few years, I would like to think I am pretty good at it now. However, if I'm learning from my friends, I should not slide first. Or if I am going to slide in, I should always reply to a story as that's a good way of making conversation, not just throw out a random 'hey you' with no context. Some of the DMs I have received are WILD, so let's dissect them.

Day 323 of asking for Only Fans

Now this one is far from the romantic DM slide I was hoping for, but I can rate them on one thing: consistency. They have sent the same DM every day for 323 days. God loves a trier, but sadly they are trying on the wrong girl.

Why hide the toes?

Again, unfortunately, this one is a no. Not much to dissect, I'm just not a foot person.

That's a trophy right there

This one I don't hate, I think it's short and simple and on the same lines as some of the ones I have used in the past.

TB to when I met my future wife

This slide came alongside a photo of when we met in Kavos in 2022. I applaud the fact he is still trying but the photo probably appeared in his memories from a year ago, and he thought he'd try his luck one more time.

Saturday night, me and you, a few drinks?

I'll be real, I like the forwardness. I think cutting to the chase and meeting up for a drink is way better than chatting online for weeks without meeting. This one is winning so far.

16 PHOTOS of his dog 'You're welcome'

Do I admit it? I smiled at this one. It didn't get a response, but like I said, dogs are the way to a girl's heart and this boy got the memo.

Overall, the DM slides I get are extremely mixed. Some I think are men who are genuinely interested, but some are clearly just wanting pictures of feet, for which I am sadly not the right person to be messaging. I think it would be quite fun to meet a partner through Instagram, but as of now, my luck is not in that department.

SEXTING

When do you think sexting should come into all of this? I think when it happens determines what outcome both parties want. If you're sexting someone straight off a DM slide, the chances are you just want to hook up with them. Of course, this could lead to something further down the line, and if it does, amazing! However, if someone slid into my DMs wanting to sext, they would stay firmly in the DMs. If you have been on a few dates, maybe three as a minimum, and the texting starts to go a little more flirtatious now that you have got to know each other more, I think this is way more exciting and almost builds up the sexual tension. I can't say I have ever sexted someone before date three unless we were just hooking up or were friends with benefits, but that's not to say you can't. It's all personal preference on timelines; there isn't a strict 'you should do this then, because this will mean this outcome', it is all different for each individual and that is the beauty of dating. Nothing is ever the same.

Holiday flings

Why is everything way more exciting when you know you're both going your separate ways at the end of the week and probably won't see each other ever again? This is the case for a lot of holiday romances, but one of my best friends, Haz, took the holiday romance seriously and is now in a relationship with him, ready to travel the world together. The story of how they met brings a smile to my face every time I tell it. It truly is like something out of a movie.

We were all on a flight to Ibiza. This is, hands down, the LAST place you would ever think you are going to meet your future boyfriend. Our trip had also been postponed twice – we were originally meant to go in June, which changed to September, then finally we got confirmed dates for October – so this is another example of what is meant for you will most definitely find you. This plane may as well have been a floating club. Everyone was up out of their seats dancing, drinking, the speaker was blaring, all we needed was some flashing lights. Haz and I got talking to a group of boys from London, they seemed funny and were all on a good level, so I spent the whole two-hour plane journey pre-drinking with them ready to go out when we landed – separately – as we never planned to bump into each other again. As we were getting ready for landing, one of the boys shouted to Haz that she was the most beautiful girl he had ever seen. Naturally, she was giggling and took the compliment but also didn't think too much about it as we never thought we would see them again. Off the back of his comment, she opened her phone and filmed a video of him sat just a few rows behind, saying, 'this boy is going to be my boyfriend', to which they both just laughed. We said our goodbyes, then went to check into our hotels.

The following night we decided we would go out as we had been working at an event all day, and would be flying home early the next morning, so the only rational option was to not sleep and to party instead. We went to one of the super clubs that holds thousands of people, so bumping into people we knew seemed like a write-off. Until a very drunk Haz spotted the boy from the plane at the bar, and we spent the whole night with them. They had their first kiss in the club and exchanged numbers, although the next morning when I showed her the photos I had taken for her she had no memory of even seeing him there. They spoke every single day when we arrived home, even throughout the six weeks we went travelling in Australia, when the time zone became a challenge. Back in the UK in January, their love story started, and they are now living together, getting ready to travel to Australia in 2024. What is so beautiful about this story is that when Haz met him, she had just left an awfully toxic relationship and was not looking for a man at ALL, but he came into her life at the exact time she needed him the most, she just didn't know it yet.

I have had a few holiday flings myself, back in the day when I used to go to Kavos and it slowly became my second home for the summer. In one of those years, I met a DJ who worked out there for the season, and even though I knew he was trouble, I liked it. What made it even better was my best friend who I was on holiday with fell for his best friend, so we went out as a two and quickly became a four, going out every night together, spending the days together, having a LOT of fun behind closed doors together. (Separately, not all four of us. I just had to clarify; I know what you were thinking!) When it was time to go home, it was just my luck that I found out he was also seeing another girl out there, and I mean, am I surprised? He could have told me I was the only one until he was blue in the face, but he might as well have had *liar* tattooed on his forehead.

That didn't stop me from being just a little gutted, as that was my first time experiencing a holiday romance, or a whirlwind romance I guess you could call it.

The only thing you need to be careful with in these situations is you must NOT catch feelings for them straight away. It is so easily done, but 90 per cent of the time it's going to end on the flight home, unless you're Haz. Another random one I had was in Magaluf, of all places. I met this boy who worked at a club we were at, and I straight away took a little fancy to him. We exchanged numbers and agreed to meet the following day for food. However, all my friends were way too drunk to continue the night and went to bed, so as I was about to sleep, he messaged me, asking if I wanted to take a bottle of wine down to the beach and go and talk. He took me to the cutest little spot, and we talked ALL night. The weirdest thing was, I knew it wasn't going to continue and nothing was going to develop from it, but even so, talking to a complete stranger about marriage, kids and both of our takes on relationships was so lovely, and this situation showed me that not every 'one-night stand' has to take place in bed.

Taking all of that into consideration now you know a little more about my experience with hook ups, I hope you can see that not all hook ups have to end with you falling in love and living happily ever after; a lot of the time it's just another frog you're going to kiss until you find your prince. I found this hard to understand in the beginning, and I used to fall for anyone who showed me the slightest bit of attention, but now I look at it all as one big learning experience and each person I have hooked up with has taught me something different about men, or even myself. Don't feel disheartened if you hook up with someone and you don't hear from them the next day, or it slowly starts to fizzle out once you have done the deed. I know it is a lot easier said than done, but that person was not *your* person if that is what is happening, and when you meet the right person they would not let the situation result in that. Have some fun, live your life and enjoy the hook ups – it's all part of the plot.

Chapter 2

The First Date

NOW WE HAVE discussed the hook-up stage, it feels only right to move on to something a little more exciting: the first date. Personally, I go through stages of loving dating and very quickly hating it. A solid 90 per cent of my dates have come from Hinge, and the other 10 per cent have come from friends of friends, but before we dissect the perfect first date, I want to share some of my dating stories, some of which are painfully tragic to write, let alone for you to read, but essential to discuss, as bad dates are inevitable and I'm sure you've all had your fair share of them too.

BOY #1 – THE HEADACHE

We're going back around three years here, to a date I have never actually told anyone about, not even my friends, because it honestly was so bizarre, I almost don't believe it happened. I matched this boy on Hinge (shock!), we got talking over message and hit it off instantly. We had so much in common, down to the exact same Starbucks orders, food orders, fashion sense; it truly was like speaking to the male version of myself. He suggested coming round my flat, to which I agreed (what is my problem with letting boys come over for a first date?). Anyway, we said we'd order food. I was honestly so excited to meet him after the text conversations, but very quickly I changed my mind. He turned up at mine with possibly the WORST attitude I have ever experienced from a boy and sat on his phone the entire time. He did not ask one question, just simply sat at my kitchen island – the opposite end to me, can I add – and responded to my questions after a few minutes of scrolling down Instagram. Just as I was getting ready to ask him to leave, because I was over this before it even began, he drops his head into his hands and claims he is having a thunderclap headache. What? It doesn't even sound real typing that out, but trust me, it is. Now if he was, fair enough, but clearly he wasn't. I very much hope he does not want to become an actor because that is one industry he would not get far in. He asked for a drink so I got him a bottle of water and two tablets, and as I handed them to him, he in return handed me his phone asking me to book him an Uber home. I gladly partook in that exchange and begged for the Uber to arrive quicker than you can say go. He got up and left without saying goodbye and I never heard from him again.

Would you even call that a date? Probably not, because I didn't learn one new thing about him; in fact, we didn't even have a conversation. It was almost as though the person I was texting was a completely different person to the boy who turned up at my house. Maybe he sent his friend instead? If you're not feeling someone, that is completely okay, but it's not okay to be so rude; simply stick it out, or politely say you need to leave.

BOY #2 – THE BLIND DATE

One of my best friends, Callum, used to live in a shared university house in Manchester with a few boys. He'd moved out at this point but had remained friends with one of them. We were out for drinks one evening and he put a photo of me on his story, and the *boy* replied asking Callum to set me up with him. I very quickly asked to see his Instagram, which Callum refused as he wanted it to be a real blind date, but he reassured me that we would really get along and we had a lot in common. I trust his opinion, so he gave the boy my number and we arranged a date. We visited a nice outdoor bar in Manchester and had some lunch, and it was so exciting and refreshing meeting up with someone unknown to me – I had no idea what he looked like, what he did for a job, nothing. I liked what I saw, and I think the excitement made me fancy him even more. We hit it off very quickly and things moved quite fast with this one. We saw each other a handful of times after this and it made me think, do I prefer blind dates to normal dates? Setting up a blind date is obviously a lot harder because it requires someone knowing someone who you might like, counting on them being single and wanting to go on a blind date too, and someone then setting it up. But in some ways it takes the nerves away because I don't know what I'm going into, it's all a surprise! If I get the opportunity, I will do one again.

BOY #3 – LET'S PLAY TOURIST

I know my friends are going to laugh at this one as I have been on two dates with different people where I have walked around London looking at the sights and both dates have failed. I always thought it would be super cute going exploring around the capital, looking at Big Ben and the London Eye, but no, both boys that I did this with, on separate occasions, of course, turned out to be seeing other girls at the same time as me. Nothing went wrong on the actual dates necessarily, as walking around gave us a lot to chat about, but both boys most definitely were not for me. They say it always comes in threes, but if I was ever asked on a sightseeing date again, the answer is an immediate no, thank you.

BOY #4 – THE ACTIVITY DATE

Finally, we are leaving the house for a Hinge Date. This was the first real activity date I had done, so I was nervous as I think it's so easy to get the ick in these situations. He booked for us to play The Cube, which I had wanted to do for ages, but I knew you had to wear these strange masks and in my head I just thought, *Oh my God, I can't see this boy in a mask on our first date.* Anyway, he put on the mask and I didn't get the ick somehow. We ended up having a fun evening and it was one of those dates where we both didn't want it to end, so we walked into town and found a cute little bar to get a drink and got very wine-drunk while sharing our deepest secrets. I think this will forever be one of my favourite dates because it was filled with so much laughter and joy – I look back and smile at this one.

BOY #5 – SETTING UP THE WORK PHONE

This is one of my most recent dates and is too funny to not put in here. Weirdly, this again was a friend of a friend who I had met several times at parties and events. Several of our friends have always said we are super similar and would make a good couple, but it was one of those where we would say we're going to see each other then we would both get busy and, truth be told, I had slept with one of his old friends so I always felt a little awkward. Putting that aside, we recently all went out to a bar, and we were glued at the hip the entire night, and he drunkenly asked if he could come round and we could order sushi and dessert. I agreed (to the second date in my living room out of these five; my flat is basically a speed-dating hot spot at this point). He arrived, half an hour late but I'll let him off, and he came in with a backpack. Now, I have always said a backpack is a bit of an ick for me – I know they are practical, but it just is not necessary on a first date, especially when he drove here so it could have been left in the boot of the car. We ate food, then moved to the sofa, where mid conversation he opens his bag and pulls out a second phone. Instantly, I thought, *Oh no, I know what a second phone means*, and was ready to get my friends to come up with a fake excuse on a phone call to get him out instantly, however, he proceeds to tell me it is his work phone for his security company. I made a joke, laughed it off and tried to continue the conversation we were having before the backpack became the third wheel, but before I know it, he is pulling out a big phone SIM receipt, and is setting up his Google Play store on a date in my living room. My eyes widened a little and I tried carrying on the conversation, but I was getting one-word responses as he was so focused on making a new password. As lovely as he was, there was just no need to do that on a date, and it was unsurprisingly very unattractive. Shockingly, I am yet to see him again.

THE EMBARRASSING ONE

When I was looking back all my dates, I was thinking surely there must be one that is somewhat embarrassing? I was correct. How did I forget, I got hit by a car. Yes, I got hit by a car. On a date. The backstory to this one is slightly weird and could be considered bad on my behalf. One of my best friends was out in Zante and had met this boy. She had a bit of a holiday fling with him, but then sent me a picture of him saying he was my type, and she was very much correct – he was beautiful. It was her idea for us both to message each other despite her having a bit of a holiday romance with him, but I got her full approval, so it was all good. Fast-forward a few weeks, we spoke on text a fair bit and then he drove to see me and spend the night. Bearing in mind he lived six hours away from Manchester, the dedication for this date was real. We went to a nice sushi restaurant because we had both spoken about how much we loved sushi, but when we started to eat with the chopsticks, he asked me how to use them. Someone who likes sushi would know how to use chopsticks, so I can't lie that this slightly gave me the ick, but we move. On the way home from the date, we were walking down one of the busiest streets in Manchester, and as we crossed the road, an Uber fully drove into the side of my leg. I wasn't injured, so it wasn't a full-on crash, but it knocked me a bit considering I was in heels. This boy just pulled me out of the way and could not stop asking if I was okay. Apart from wishing the ground would open and swallow me there and then, I was fine, no bruises or anything. He left the next day and proceeded to message me, so he didn't get the ick. I'll be honest, if it was the other way around; I would have gotten the ick, and I got the ick about it happening to myself! I politely told him I didn't think it was going to work out, more so because of my severe embarrassment, as he was a lovely boy.

How do I make the first move?

Making the first move and moving from a dating app to a first date shouldn't, in an ideal world, be hard. I prefer it when a guy straight up asks me on a date or to see me in person, because then there is no getting to know each other on text, falling in love too quickly and ending up with a thunderclap headache when you finally meet. It is also way easier to meet up quicker, because then you can ask all your questions in person and the conversation will generally just flow better. If you're struggling to find someone who will jump straight to it and instead wants to chat over text for a while, here are a few tips to ensure it doesn't just remain on message.

1. Be bold and make the first move! I'm a little bit of a hypocrite in this case, as I would personally way prefer the guy to ask me on a date first. However, it's 2024; women can make the first move and that is okay.
2. The two-week mark. I have a personal rule with this as I think if anything is going to move forward, you need to meet within the first two weeks of matching or speaking to each other. There are several reasons for this, the first being you will get to know each other so well within those two weeks that meeting up after that will most likely make you more nervous as you already know so much about each other, now what do you talk about? The first date is so exciting because you are finding out different things about each other and it's so much more fun and intimate when done in person! Also, after a few days of talking you will know if you want to see someone or if you see nothing progressing from it, so there is no point texting each other for weeks getting your hopes up, only to meet in person and for it to not be all that it seemed.
3. Don't be afraid of a phone call. I have FaceTimed boys before meeting them and sometimes it's a

nice way to break the ice and hear their voice! This could lead to a real-life date sooner than you think.

THE PHONE CALL

Leading on from tip number three, do you think a phone call is a good idea before a date? I think it's actually a very good thing that shows time and effort required from both you and the boy and enables you to get to know each other that little bit more before meeting, creating even more excitement for your first date. I did this with my ex-boyfriend. We matched on Hinge, and we arranged a date, which I then cancelled because I was too nervous, even though I told him something had come up. So yes, I lied . . . it happens to the best of us. He asked to FaceTime me, and I still remember the giddy, happy feeling you get when you see they are calling. We spoke on the phone for around half an hour and then at the end of the call we arranged a date to meet in person. I felt *so* much better doing it this way as I automatically felt that bit more comfortable around him, so when it came to meeting him, I was more excited than nervous, and I attended the date that time instead of lying and saying I was busy due to nerves.

However, I do see that this is not always the best way

to go about it, and it can be some people's worst nightmare to have to speak to someone on the phone before meeting them in person, and that's okay! Everyone is different when it comes down to dating, and sometimes it's a little trial and error process. You try calling someone, you don't like it and realise you prefer to wait until the first date to speak? No problem, that's what you do next time! I also think it depends on the type of boy you're speaking to, because some boys don't use their phones as much as you'd think and would prefer to meet in person.

WITHOUT A TIME, THERE IS NO DATE

I have spoken to my fair share of boys now within the seven or so years that I've been dating and one thing I have learnt is that effort is everything, and the right person will make that effort.

I was in a sticky situationship a few years ago (which I will speak about in more depth later in the book) in which I really experienced the bare minimum of effort. However, it took me a few months to realise that I was most definitely settling, and I deserved more. It's funny how the human brain works, or maybe it is just my brain, but as soon as you catch feelings for someone it's almost as though you would do anything to ensure that person is happy, because their happiness becomes your priority – sadly sometimes over your own. This boy didn't ask to take me out on a date outside of the house until we had been speaking for two and a half months. Yes, you read that right: two and a half months. Our first date was inside the house – and so was the second, and third, and so on. Old me would have said there is nothing wrong with this, but now I know there is most definitely something wrong with this. Why did he not want to take me out? Was he keeping secrets? Did he not want to be seen with me? Was he seeing someone else and didn't want them to find out about me? Spoiler alert for the full story: it was a combination of all three.

From this situation, I realised that I deserved to be taken out, I deserved to have effort put into me, and I deserve more than the bare minimum. Once I started taking care of my own emotions and recognising the situation I was in wasn't healthy, but most importantly wasn't making me happy, I removed myself from it. Fast-forward a few months and I met a brand-new boy, who would not stop asking until I agreed to go on a date with him. I experienced all girls' dreams of 'I'll pick you up at 7pm, be ready' and *this*, ladies and gentlemen, is what I deserved. I felt appreciated, like I finally was someone's priority, and it made me reflect on the situation I was in before and in some way upset me. I was sad that I had allowed myself to be someone's option, because I should have loved myself enough previously to get up and leave. But when you like someone, I know this is a lot easier said than done.

Just to make this point clear, this is in no way about money, and a boy does not need to take you to the most expensive restaurant and buy you dinner with a fancy bottle of wine to show you that he cares. He could suggest a walk in the park, write down on a piece of paper ten things he likes about you, or turn up at your door with your favourite chocolate. The point I'm leaning towards here is that *effort is everything*. When a boy really likes you, the effort will be there and will be clear; you won't have to wonder if he wants to see you or if he likes you. When he likes you, there will always be a next time for your next date.

Where should we go for our first date?

Now I have laid down the rules of what to expect when you are dating, let's talk date ideas. Each person is going to have a different preference regarding what they would like to do, but these would be my top five ideas for the perfect date . . .

1. Drinks in a bar – Cute and casual but you can take it as far as you wish. Do you have a few drinks then say goodnight and go home, or do you enjoy each other's company so much you want to do a bar hop and stay out together all night?
2. Dinner – This is sometimes a little heavy for a first date, as in all honesty there is not a chance I'm attempting to eat spaghetti Bolognese or a burger in front of anyone I've just met, let alone my date, but if you don't care about any of that, go for it. Eat your heart out, girl!
3. The activity – An easy go-to would be mini golf or bowling, because it gives you something else to focus on other than just the conversation of getting to know each other. If you're feeling extra nervous but okay about potentially getting the ick if they must wear bowling shoes or swing the golf club and miss the ball, this one is for you.
4. A creative day – I have never done a date like this, but I think it would be so fun to do a pottery date or a cooking class! I guess this is a tamer version of an activity date, as this lowers the risk of

embarrassing yourself and means you can ask your date for help as a bonding moment ... Just a tip!

5. The holiday – Don't tell me you have not thought about matching with someone on a dating app, hitting it off instantly and deciding to spontaneously book a date abroad? Now, of course, you need to be careful they aren't a catfish in this situation, so a FaceTime or a phone call before would be top priority, but how fun to go away for the weekend with someone you've never met and explore a new city with them? Of course, if you are going to do this, you have to do it in a safe way. Ensure that you have told your friends or family where you are going and who you are going with, and maybe even book separate hotel rooms, just so you still have your personal space whilst being away with them.

Dating is different depending on where you live

Yes, I have weirdly found this to be true. I moved up to Manchester in 2020 and started dating later that year and, wow, the difference between dating in the north and in the south is crazy. The differences are hard to explicitly define, but what I now know is dating up north is way more successful for me.

Dating apps were my only real option when I was living back home; I left school and no one had caught my eye there, and I lived in a very small town. I would often go to London on dates if I was going to see someone, but as you read earlier with my date example of boy #3, none of those were typically success stories. I just found that dating in London was a lot more serious, I guess. The go-to date in London would be getting a drink at a bar, as it's always so busy and everyone works all day, and the streets of Soho after 6pm on a weekday are a fun vibe if you are meeting someone for the first time, but I always felt as though people who lived in London just did not want to date. I would speak to so many different people on dating apps, but nothing would ever move on from the app, and I was annoyingly too stubborn to ask them on a first date. But like I said, if he wanted to, he would.

There is a dating app that is London-based called Thursday, which only works on a Thursday. Their tagline is #BetterInPerson and they encourage people to match, chat and meet up on the same day – Thursday! I love this because you just cut straight to the chase and if you don't like the person when you meet them, great, no time wasted texting and onto the next. But if you do like them, now you can exchange numbers – and this is where it gets exciting. There's no two-week rule in sight here.

They also host events on a Thursday at different spots around London that will be filled with single people, so it's almost like a speed-dating situation, but less stressful as you won't be sat at a table waiting for the next person every few minutes. You can walk around and speak to whoever you fancy, knowing that you will all be there for the same reason: you're so done with dating apps and you want to just have that cute story of bumping into each other in a bar and falling madly in love. I am yet to go to one of these events so I'm not sure what type of men go, however ...

Okay, hold up. I admit, I did it. My excuse for going to one of these events was market research, okay? I had to do it for all of you reading the book ... it's only right. Now, I was not expecting to say this, but I think this might be one of my new favourite ways to date. Technically, it is still meeting someone through a dating app, however, it really does not feel like that because you are seeing everyone in person, and you know that everyone is there for the same reason. Unless the odd person is just looking for one night of fun, you can be pretty confident that everyone at these events is looking for something that might develop into a relationship, otherwise why would you go through all the effort of going to one of these events? If you wanted some fun, you would just go out to a night club, right?

Anyway, let's talk about the type of people that were there. It is in London, so it was giving businessman – a lot of suits, quarter-zips and some painfully tight trousers. Someone who caught my eye had very cool fashion sense – cargo trousers, baggy jumper, lots of jewellery, trainers I was into – but I didn't get a chance to speak to him, which was a shame. Everyone was super friendly and very confident, which I liked because I was quite nervous to go up and speak to people, but once someone would come over and the conversation would start to flow, I really started to enjoy myself and I must admit, I wondered why I had not come to an event like that before. The only thing I got a bit bored with was having several repetitive conversations of 'Hello, what is your name, what do you do for a job?', just because it felt like I was on repeat, almost like a robot. But of course you must have those sorts of conversations to begin with, because if you were scrolling on a dating app, these are the things you would first get to look at before you decided whether you were going to swipe or match them.

Overall, would I go to one of these events again? Absolutely. I think it is an incredible way to meet people who are on the same wavelength as you. It is a nice excuse to get yourself out there and meet people and is less pressure than organising a one-to-one date on a dating app with someone and being very nervous. If anyone reading this has met a partner and is now with them through one of these events, don't be shy, drop me a message or DM with the story of how it went and how it is going now. I love hearing different people's experiences and getting some suggestions on how I could approach my next dating event in a similar way.

However, I still think dating in Manchester is just better. Hinge is way friendlier up north, and as I live very central I turn my distance to the lowest it can go, so everyone I have dated has lived in my area, which is either a really good thing because I can see them all of the time or whenever I want, but also a bad thing because I now have dated someone in nearly every building I can see out of my window, so I know I am bound to bump into them again at some point. I'm not sure whether it is just living in a city that makes it easier than dating down south, but I have found that up north people are a lot more fun and open to dating, and you can have one of those wild, crazy nights out with someone you've just met and it won't be awkward. Also, the men in Manchester are, indeed, chef's kiss. Saffron would agree with me on this one too: before she was in a relationship, she came up to Manchester for the weekend and we went on a night out together, and she hand-on-heart says they are some of the best-looking boys she has ever seen and would move here in a heartbeat if she could.

Now the funny thing about dating in Manchester for the last few years is that I have now figured out where to go to meet a certain type of man. So, this is your guide to dating in Manchester.

Albert's Schloss – Everyone's favourite social bar in the heart of Deansgate. If you visit this bar on a Thursday after 7pm, you will be greeted by every man who works in a bank or in compliance, wearing work shirts and tight trousers. If you are looking for this type of man, you're in luck. I have experienced this a few times and met some hilarious people, but if you are looking for someone who has a personality outside of a nine-to-five office, I'd avoid this one at all costs. The live music is 10/10, though, so there's always that.

Manhatta – This one is a nice vibrant bar just down the road from Albert's Schloss but is filled with university students and younger people. The drinks are good and I like the R&B music, however, I think this one is more for a quick hook up – nothing serious is making it out of this bar.

Northern Quarter – Now this is the slightly edgier area of Manchester where everyone is just there for fun. No fights, no stuck-up CEOs, just people wanting a good time. There is a good club here called Lost in Tokyo if you fancy a dance, but there are SO many cool bars, like Blockbuster, a bar themed from the old Blockbuster rent-a-movie store, serving movie-themed cocktails. You'll also notice skinny jeans don't exist in this area of town; it is baggy jean and plaid shirt central, so if that is your go-to style on a man, head to this end.

Diecast – This is one of the newest bars in Manchester and gives the cool people vibe. Dress is very street style, and everyone looks almost the same, as if someone has copied and pasted the same boy in cargos and a Represent tee, but this is my type so I will stay here, I think. They have dancers that do a show every hour or so above the bar and they have around 15 daiquiri slushy machines, so it's a cool bar to try out. However, enter with caution if you are active on dating apps; I went on opening night and bumped into four people I have either spoken to, been ghosted by, kissed or wanted to kiss – but the upside is if you go here you are bound to have a good night!

MNKY HSE – Just a heads up, you aren't meeting a boyfriend here. This club is so fun for a night out and a hook up, but anything more than that I would highly doubt. This is giving skinny jeans and polo necks, so if that's your type, get this on your itinerary. Oh, and if you like a footballer, you are most likely to spot one in China White, as they often go here on weekends.

These are five very popular locations in Manchester to meet someone at but also to visit for a date. However, there are also a few secret, hidden gems that would be perfect if you want something a little more low-key . . .

The Washhouse – This is one of my favourite cocktail bars in Manchester because you would have NO idea it is there – it's a speakeasy! Speakeasys are bars that look completely different on the outside so you would never guess they are bars. As the name suggests, The Washhouse is disguised as a launderette, with lots of washing machines, and on the wall is a phone. You pick up the phone and ask to collect your washing under your name and one of the washing machine doors will open for you to enter the bar. The cocktail menu here is endless, they even have Coco Pop vodka served with a bowl of actual Coco Pops for you to eat whilst drinking, and they have a slide from the top of the bar down to the bottom, as well as a party button in the toilets. This bar is so fun for a date as you can use the cocktail menu as an incredible conversation starter, and it also has romantic vibes, because you can sit at individual candlelit tables.

Alcotraz: Cell Block Three-Four – An immersive experience is always fun if you want to have a few drinks with someone and see where the night will take you. Here, you sit in a cell block, bring your own alcohol, and hand it to the wardens to mix you a strange cocktail, all while watching a show. Top tip for this place: you WILL be drunk and you won't remember the rest of the night, as they don't mess with the measurements here.

Saffron's take

I wouldn't say I particularly prefer any one of these venues over the other, but in the past when I've been on nights out in Manchester it has been easier to chat to people as it's not my home town. I'm not worried I'll bump into someone I know, and I feel a bit more at ease and therefore more confident as a result. Anastasia has taken me out to several places but one of my favourites must be Albert's Schloss. She told me about this place before I came up to visit and it really did not disappoint. The whole vibe and atmosphere of the place is perfect whether you are going on a single girls' night out with your friends or with a date! I love live music, so if you love that too, you need to give this place a try.

Saffron Barker

What do we talk about?

Now you have got a time and a date, you need the conversation. I love it when the chat is even – you're both asking the same number of questions and it's not one-sided. So here are a few of my favourite topics for a first date.

- **Favourite drink and cocktail** Find out what you each like and try each other's drink if they are different. If you're both feeling adventurous, you could order a drink for each other as a surprise and see if they like it. Just a nice light-hearted way of making conversation but still keeping the chat fun.
- **If you could get on a plane to anywhere right now, where would you go?** Travel is a classic go-to subject for a date. Find out their dream places to visit and where they have already visited, then compare. Discuss what you loved about the place, what you hated, then if you agree on the same destination, maybe you can visit it together for a future date.
- **What is something I would never guess about you?** I like this one as it encourages you both to be more open and share things beyond the classic, surface-level

stuff. This is your time to show your hidden talent, or something that no one else knows about you.

- **If you suddenly had one billion pounds, what would you do with it?** I think this can tell you a lot about a person, and again goes a little deeper. It begins a conversation that can turn into a healthy debate, so you can see another side to them early on.
- **If you could have dinner with three people, dead or alive, who would it be?** This is one of my favourite questions ever to ask on a date. I love hearing people's answers because it shows you their interests and what sort of people they are drawn to. Again, this can be a full-blown conversation starter and not just a quick question, so make sure your drink is full to the top before you ask it.
- **What is one thing you want to accomplish before you die?** This one is for when you are a few drinks in, as it can get deep, but I think it's always interesting to ask this as I love someone who is ambitious and has big goals, so their answer is key for me.
- **If you had no obligations, what would your perfect day look like?** Now, if they are clever, or feeling flirty from all the cocktails, they will find a way to include you in this answer. It's nice seeing what people like to do in their spare time as I think it tells you a lot

about them, but this way you can start to flirt, if that is what you want. And if he doesn't include you in the answer, simply ask why as you stare into his eyes. This works every time.

- **What music album or artist has impacted your life?** It's common for an album to have impacted a person in some way and it's even better when you both listen to the same music and can relate to it. If you don't listen to the music your date likes, try not to panic, this just means you have a whole new genre to try out and listen to – with him.

- **If you were to write a book, what would it be about?** This is a fun one for me to answer as I would simply turn around and say, 'Well, men.' This would open a never-ending, black-hole conversation and probably lead him to think I was there for research. Of course, I would tell him otherwise, but he's not wrong! I like this question because some people would prefer to write a story rather than make it about them, and I think you can tell a lot about someone through their answer to this.

- **If you could have any superpower, what would it be?** A nice light-hearted one if you are running out of questions to ask but want to keep the conversation flowing. It's always fun finding out whether someone would prefer to be able to fly or read minds.

- **What's the most spontaneous thing you have ever done?** Spontaneity is one of my key things to look for in a man, so if they say they have booked a flight and gone the next day, we love that, as it shows they are adventurous and spontaneous! But if they say their version of spontaneous is trying hot at Nando's instead of medium, we have a problem.
- **A game.** If the worst comes to the worst, play a game! Never have I ever, would you rather?, piccolo. Just be prepared for it to potentially turn sexual and to hear some answers you may not want to hear from someone you have only just met.

If you are with someone who is super chatty, these tips should be perfect for you. I think it's always best to come prepared with a list of questions just in case the other person is nervous, then these will ease you both into a conversation without it feeling too forced. However, there are also *many* topics that should be avoided on a first date. There is getting to know someone, then there is getting to *know* someone, and some things are better left until you are a few dates in, like . . .

- **The ex conversation** – I don't think it is a bad thing to briefly and succinctly bring up when you were last seeing someone, or were last in a relationship, as that gives the other person a little idea of how ready or not you are for things and what speed you like to go at. However, if they are asking what your ex was like, are describing their ex or saying bad things about what their ex has done to them, this is a huge no. The point of dating is because you are no longer with that person and if they feel the need to bring them up, then as sad as it is, they are not over that person and not ready to move forward with you.

- **Avoid it being one-sided** – I have been on a few dates in the past where the conversation has been very one-sided, and it has massively put me off. If they are asking you a question, it's SO easy to flip it round and ask, 'How about you?' If you are asking them a question and once they are done speaking they go silent and don't ask you a question back, continue with caution.

Now, if any of these situations occur, or you are just not enjoying yourself, every girl needs a locker of excuses in the back of their mind that they can use to get out of a date. As much as I hate admitting this, I have lied before to bring a date to a halt. Well, this technically went a little further than a date; my friends and I went out for drinks and then he came and met us when we had already been out for a while. We carried on having drinks, and he asked to stay at mine. Now, I know what you're thinking, we did not sleep together, but I really did not want him around the next day. Once I've been drinking, I am so ready for a solo day after and he was not taking that from me! So I lied and said I had a train to catch at 12:30. He got up and left around 11am, but first he offered to take me to the train station and was not accepting no as my answer, so I continued the lie and said I was getting picked up by my friend who I was going with. It worked, and the only place I travelled to that day was downstairs to pick up my food delivery and straight back to bed. He still to this day does not know that I lied to get out of that one, so if you're reading this, I am genuinely so sorry, but I just wanted my own space.

If you want to get out of a date before they end up back at your house, I've got a few excuses you can throw his way.

The emoji – This isn't technically a direct excuse from you, this one is coming from your friends, so it is up to their wildest imagination. When I go on a date, I always tell my friends, and if it is going badly, I will just message them ANY emoji, and they know that it is a code-red situation and they need to get me out at their earliest convenience. The reason I say an emoji – and any emoji – is because this is easier than having to type out a full-blown word at the table and getting your phone out can be done slyly so the other person can't see. Ten minutes later you're getting a phone call – your best friend's cat has died so you've got to go, what a shame!

The work emergency – Oh no, there has been an emergency at work? I guess I should probably go handle it. If your date is on a weekend this one may not be as straightforward, but if it's work, you can't really say no.

You have plans, remember? – You genuinely could have last-minute plans that you have forgotten about, so this one is always a good one to use. If you don't and it's a lie, message your friends and arrange something! You're already ready and dressed now, you may as well continue the night with someone else.

The headache – Again, I feel like this is somewhat believable. You suddenly have a headache, and you need to leave. The other person can't really argue with this one, as if you have a headache, you're not going to be in the mood to talk, annoyingly.

Just be HONEST – Depends how brutal or ballsy you're feeling, but you could just be honest and say you don't think the date is going how you want it to go. As harsh as this would be and almost embarrassing in the moment, I think it's actually very important to be honest as there's no time wasted, and the other person will at least know the truth instead of feeling like they have been lied to. Not the easiest of excuses, but arguably the best one.

The double date

I absolutely love a good double date. Would you ever go on one as a first date? I think I would if I was going with my best friend. Earlier in this book when I mentioned Saffron and I both speaking to twins, this would have been the perfect situation for a double date, but sadly the bag got fumbled in that case. Before Saff got into a relationship, I was always on the lookout for two boy best friends or brothers that we could date, as us two have never done a double date together. When I was with my ex-boyfriend, I went on a double date with him and one of my best friends, Haz, and her boyfriend, the couple who met on the plane to Ibiza! That was so much fun, we spent the whole Sunday together and went for a roast dinner – we are all massive foodies so this worked perfectly for us – then we downed a bottle of wine between us and headed to an escape room. Doing an escape room after a bottle of wine was an experience! We did escape, so the wine can't have hit us as much as we believed.

I also did another double date with one of my situationships and Byron and his ex-boyfriend, which now I think about it is slightly odd as I just remembered we also went for a roast. Clearly, a roast dinner is the perfect setting for a nice double date.

As you are probably aware, I have been on my fair share of dates over the years, but the funniest part about going on dates is the messages that I send to my best friends when I get back or they leave. I honestly am the worst person to speak to directly after a date because I will most probably declare that I have fallen in love with them and they are the love of my life, when I can tell you none of them have been this and I wake up the next day in a completely different head space. When the adrenaline is still high and I'm in my excited stage, these are some of the messages I have sent to people in my phone . . .

Date #1

Anastasia
'He's outside.'
'He's beautiful.'

Byron
'OMG we love this for you!! Have fun and be safe pls.'

Anastasia
'He's unreal, I'm going to die, I'm in love with him.'

I told you, the 'I'm in love with him' is a common theme throughout these messages.

Date #2

Anastasia
'Babe, I just got back.'

Saffron
'How did it go?'

Anastasia
'It's so weird we are the EXACT same person and imagine I got into the car and on the seat was flowers!!'

Saffron
'OMG you said you wanted flowers. Stop, this is so cute.'

This last one was the sweetest date. We had been for our first date in a bar in the Northern Quarter, and in all honesty I was a little sceptical about going on date #2 because he was on the quiet side, which there is nothing wrong with but I rely on the other person being able to banter me back, and I felt we lacked this. But I thought I'd go and see him again because, why not? On our second date, he had remembered that I had told him I like to go and look at big houses (don't ask why, just dreaming of what I would love to have one day), so he picked me up, with a big bouquet of flowers on the passenger seat – from a proper florist, not just from a shop – and drove me to the McDonald's drive-thru to order me what I told him my favourite meal was on date #1. Certified passenger princess. I am so glad I went on this second date because he opened up so much more, and it really made me realise how much he had listened to me on the first, so even though he was quiet and technically a little more introverted than me, he paid attention, which is such a beautiful quality for a boy to have.

Date #3

Anastasia
'I just got back, he is BEAUTIFUL, easily the best-looking person I have ever been on a date with.'

Byron
'Please don't get obsessed this quickly again.'

> **Anastasia**
> 'I won't, but I want him to meet you all, already I don't know what is going on.'

I can confirm he did not in fact meet my friends and I got the ick. I gave myself the ick in this situation and I really wish I hadn't because this is very shallow of me, but we all have our weird ones and we don't shame here. He wasn't the tallest of boys, but he wasn't the shortest, I just have a weirdly shaped sofa, and when he was sat leaning on the back of it his feet couldn't touch the floor and he honestly looked about four years old. I feel AWFUL even typing this, but I have an image in my head that my brain may have warped, so it might not be as bad as I'm imagining, but I just can't move past it. They do say you can't get the ick with the right person, though, so he clearly just wasn't the one.

Message #4 – Pre-date

Saffron
'ANNA!! Guess what?'

Anastasia
'WHAT? Has he asked you on a date yet?'

Saffron
'FINALLY!! What should I say?'

For context here, this was before Saffron had got into a relationship and she matched this boy on Hinge who she had been speaking to for just over a week. Normally, she is a straight-to-the-point girl; she doesn't like messaging and would much rather meet up in person so no time is wasted if she doesn't like them. However, she and this boy were basically the male and female versions of each other, and she couldn't quite believe that his go-to drink was Monster mixed with vodka, so she let it slide that he was yet to ask her on a date. This evening he finally messaged her asking when he could see her, and I instantly knew that was what she was going to say to me. I guess I just have that best-friend instinct!

> **Anastasia**
> 'Say you're free before we go away because it's going to be a few weeks otherwise and you want to see him before we leave.'

> **Saffron**
> 'Okay I'll just put Friday?'

Turns out he wasn't free before we went on holiday. Boring.

As you can see from the four examples, I am the WORST for getting excited after a date, to the point where when I do go on a date with someone who it genuinely works out with, none of my friends are going to believe me because I say the same thing every single time I meet a boy. As I'm writing this book, I'm learning a lot about myself, and one main tip I am taking from this is to not say I am in love next time I get home from spending three hours with someone, but to wait and take it slow. I'm excited to go on my next first date. Getting older, I am gaining more clarity on what I want in a boyfriend, and I'm not just dating to hook up anymore, I am dating to find a partner, someone I can share my life with and, as scary as it sounds, someone to hopefully marry and start a family with. Even though the thought of being with one person is terrifying because all I have ever known is dating and messing around, I look forward to meeting the person who is going to change all of that for me and, who knows, they might just be a few swipes away on a dating app.

Chapter 3
Red Flags and Warning Signs

RED FLAGS. I honestly believe every single person you date will have one of these. You can be dating someone for four years and never have an argument or a problem, but nobody is perfect and there is always going to be something that will need work, or compromise. You could technically call this a beige flag, as red flags tend to be non-negotiable.

I have experienced SO many red flags within my

dating experiences. Here are a few of the standout ones I have seen, and that you should look out for . . .

1. **They are controlling over what you wear.**
   This one is unfortunately so common, and so wrong. It is YOUR body, and you should wear whatever you want to wear. I will never understand the whole 'cover up you're showing too much cleavage', or 'that dress is too short'. Looking into this on a deeper level, it screams insecurity from the boy's side, and they should be proud that you are out with them. So what if a few other people stare at you on your night out or compliment you? If there is trust in the relationship, you won't act on anything, and your boyfriend should be proud that you are indeed his and no one else's. Never let a boy make you feel bad for wearing what you want to wear; a man would never do that.
2. **They make you second guess their feelings.**
   This is one of the biggest red flags to look out for because no man should ever make you second guess how they feel about you – you should always know. Of course, in the beginning it can take a while to figure out exactly how you are feeling; however, if this continues into months of dating and every

time you leave a date with this person you're having to think to yourself, Does he like me? that is your sign to leave. I have been in this situation before and it took me a few months to finally pluck up the courage to walk away. Now, having experienced those feelings of self-doubt, I know I will never allow a boy to make me feel like that again.

3. **They don't tell their friends about you.**

    This one is more of a dating red flag. From getting to know me so far in this book, you will know I love to tell my friends about my dates, the boys I am seeing and all the dirty details. Of course, I understand that not everyone is as open as I like to be, but if you have been dating someone for a few months and he has not told his friends about you, or you have not met any of his friends, something fishy may be going on, or there may be someone else on the scene alongside you. If someone likes someone, they want them to meet their friends and show them off, not the opposite, so if you still haven't met their friends or spoken to them over the phone by the two-month mark, I would class this as a red flag.

4. **The jealousy scale.**

    Now, I'll say it for all of us, we love a bit of jealousy sometimes, as it shows you that they care and it makes you feel wanted – sometimes it might even turn you on, if you're into that. But there is a scale when it comes to jealousy, and there comes a point where jealousy turns into possessiveness, and it gets unhealthy. If your other half doesn't want you to have male friends because he is jealous, or he won't let you talk to other boys on a night out even if it is no more than a conversation, this is where the jealousy goes too far. Again, this is nothing but a reflection of themselves, because if they were comfortable and confident enough in themselves and the relationship, it shouldn't be a problem. Never let a boy's hint of jealousy turn sour. Stand your ground and know when enough is enough.

5. **Gaslighting.**

Someone who is gaslighting you will constantly trivialise your thoughts and feelings. When they pull out the 'this is all your fault' or 'you're being too sensitive' card, no you are not and no it is not your fault. This can make you feel so isolated; the power balance in a relationship should always be 50/50, but this kind of behaviour throws that right off scale. It becomes worse when you begin to believe them and you start to think it is your fault, or you are being too sensitive, because then you will change the way you are acting, and you never need to change for anyone, especially a man. I think this is one of the worst red flags. It's very common to carry past experiences of relationships with you into new ones, and this sort of behaviour sticks with someone and can affect future partnerships as it's how your brain has been conditioned to think it's a normal way to act. If you notice any form of this, even just slightly, bring it up straight away to your partner, and talk it out.

Red flags are the worst of the worst and tend to stop a relationship from progressing or can bring them to an end. But there are also beige flags, which I mentioned earlier. These aren't quite as bad as red flags; they are more like character quirks that could be seen as cute in some instances or something that could nearly give you the ick.

Here are some examples:

- Not turning off the lights when leaving the house.
- Leaving the car to run out of petrol before putting more in.
- Always leaving the house with no phone charge.
- Never asking details because they are unbothered about anything and everything.

- Only wearing socks with holes in and refusing to buy any new ones.

These are by no means red flags, and if they really wanted to the person could deal with them. Personally, I think they are so funny, and I would love my partner to have a few beige flags. I think these are the things that even though they annoy you, they are one of many reasons why you love that person, because it makes them who they are and different to someone else. I might start asking what people's beige flags are on first dates – it's a good conversation starter if they have never heard of them before and it could uncover a few funny secrets or stories about them.

Horror dating stories

On top of the thunderclap headache date and the guy who thought it was time to set up his new phone, I have, sadly, had more dates that have not worked out, and so have my friends.

This guy I was dating a few years ago was so lovely, and honestly the last person I would ever expect to do what happened in this next story, but I guess it is always the ones you least expect. We had been going to the same house parties and after three or four meetings, he finally asked one of my friends if I was interested in him, to which I quickly responded yes! (I had been interested since the first time we met, I was just too scared to make the first move!)

He took me on a date to a cute outdoor drinking place and it went on from there. Over around five weeks we spent a lot of time together and it got intense very quickly. Fast-forward to another one of those house parties, but this time it was at a huge house filled with lots of people I didn't know, so I stuck with him and his best friend. I thought something weird was going on when his best friend was the one messaging me asking me where I was if I had been gone for longer than five minutes, rather than him, but me being young and obsessed, I looked past it. We left this house and went back to their apartment with a group of people, and the boy I was meant to be dating just suddenly disappeared. I hadn't got a clue where he had gone, and he wasn't responding to any of my messages. Around an hour went by, then his best friend came over and asked me if I was okay. I said yes, I was just wondering where said boy was, to which his best friend decided to break the news to me that he had gone upstairs to a different floor, to go and sleep with his ex. I had NO idea that his ex was even in the building, let alone that he was still in contact with her to arrange occasions like this. Don't hate me for this part, but the anger took over, and his best friend was making moves on me, so I just didn't stop it. Truthfully, I had always fancied his best friend but that was kept on the downlow when I was with him, so the situation ended up working in my favour, and as much as it had initially annoyed me, I got the boy I wanted. Yes, I know, I did the classic 'got with his best friend to piss him off move' but despite it working, I ended up preferring his best friend, until he also f***ed me over. But that's a story for later in the book . . .

I'm not the only one with some dating horror stories. One of my friends has in fact been catfished. He used Grindr to arrange a date, which might have been the first mistake, but each to their own, I suppose. The guy's pictures were very attractive, and he was excited to meet him. When he got to the meeting place, my friend was stood waiting and the man walked over to him and introduced himself. He was not the man my friend was meant to be meeting. In that situation, what do you even do? Did the person use someone else's pictures because they have no confidence, or was it because they have an ulterior motive? My friend couldn't decide, so he stood and spoke to him for ten or so minutes, then said he needed the bathroom and upped and left. I honestly don't blame him, as catfishing is a scary thing, and you never know someone's intention with it. (If you are ever in that situation, one of my date excuses from Chapter 2 should help you out.)

Do you want to know what the worst dating story of them all is? My mum's. My mum has been single now for around nine years, but she has lived in her time, and she has also gone on some very interesting dates. One memorable one that she told me about was when she was around my age, and she was dating someone who proposed to her – the difference in our situations at the same age is truly astounding. She had an inkling that something was off one night after they had been on a date, so she decided to follow him home. I can't defend this behaviour, but I wasn't even born when this happened so who am I to comment? He went inside his flat, and my mum, being in a very drunken state, thought it would be fun to enter the property through the window, not the front door. He, however, lived on the first floor, roughly six metres high, so she climbed up the drainpipe, like a secret agent on a life-or-death mission, managed to look through his window where nothing fishy was even going on, and instead of climbing back down, fell flat onto concrete. As she was drunk she didn't feel the pain and the adrenaline probably took over her body, but the next morning she woke up screaming in pain and could not move her back. My nan called an ambulance and turned out she had in fact broken two discs in her lower back and she was laid out flat in hospital for weeks.

There are several lessons to be taken from this horror of a date: one, drink responsibly; and two, if you don't trust a man, just wait until the next day to speak to him and knock on his front door.

Ghosting

I'm not proud to say I have ghosted someone. When I did it I hadn't experienced it myself, so I had no idea how it would feel, but having had it done to me now, I would never do it again. I have learnt that is it kinder to give someone an explanation, no matter how much that may upset them, because giving them a reason can give them closure, otherwise you're letting them sit around, waiting for a reply that isn't going to come, and that's only going to upset them and cause them to question their worth and think it was all their fault.

It really was not my proudest moment. I had been on two dates with this guy, and he was actually very sweet, so I'm not entirely sure, looking back, why I ghosted him. I have a little internal issue that as soon as something goes well, I like to self-sabotage, so I guess this was my version of doing that. He even double messaged, and I still never replied. A reply that would have taken me one minute to write out and explain, but I let him wonder for a little longer than a minute, and for that I can only apologise.

After this, I then got ghosted a few times. Was it karma for me ghosting someone? Possibly. The first one was someone I had matched with on Raya. We hadn't met, just spoken online, but for some reason I really took to him. I imagined our full life together, which is such a me thing to do, and then after around a week of speaking, I just never heard from him again. I was gutted for a few days as I find it hard to meet someone that I'm attracted to – I guess I'm just very picky – but I really did think he was beautiful, so it's a shame that one never worked out.

The other time I got ghosted is the story I explained in Chapter 1. Remember the guy who got weirded out because I matched with one of his friends? Well, the plot thickens. I was scrolling through my Hinge a few days after he didn't reply, and I came across another one of his friends. The reason I know this was one of his friends was because they were all in each other's photos, and his prompts were similar, now I'm thinking about it. The guy who ghosted me was a dermatologist, so his prompts were about his skincare, and so was his friend's – get some originality, boys. Anyway, I swallowed my pride, screenshot the friend, sent it to the boy and as a joke, said I had found another one of his friends. He replied instantly, and we had a full conversation which for some reason turned very sexual, I'm unsure how. We were up speaking for a few hours and then he fell asleep so didn't reply. I woke up the next morning and he was still yet to reply, so I accepted defeat. However, it got to lunch time and I had a reply, so maybe I wasn't being ghosted after all? We spoke for a few more days, and the day before I went to Ibiza on holiday, he decided to ghost me again. I mean, just in time for a holiday, so I used it as an excuse to go a little wild but like, really? Twice by the same boy?

A few weeks passed and I heard nothing, so I just left it at that. Until I was lying in bed one night and I begin to get an array of unknown numbers call me. I answered, and it was first a girl saying that this boy who had ghosted me had given her my number. I put the phone down, very confused at this point, and a few minutes later I get another phone call, this time it was a boy saying the exact same thing. I lay in bed a little freaked out if I'm honest, so I decided to swallow my pride, AGAIN, and message him to ask him to stop giving out my number. He again replied instantly, claiming he had also just been called and it was someone telling him they knew where he lived. I'm not sure how much I believe of that, I just don't think he expected a text from me that night, so got a little embarrassed and tried to cover up what had happened. I made a joke about him ignoring me, and he claimed he got 'cold feet'. When I asked why, I got ghosted. Again. This time, I am accepting the loss and never messaging this boy again. In all fairness, I don't think it really is a loss on my behalf, if he couldn't give me an explanation and instead decided to hand out my number, that says a lot more about him than it does me.

Toxic behaviour

Red flags, ghosting, sleeping with your ex, all the things I have spoken about in this chapter could technically be classed as toxic. I have been in situations where I am aware that they are toxic, but the naive part inside me thinks I can change the guy and almost fix him. Let me tell you now, you will never be able to fix or change a man, unless they *want* to change for you.

Lying is another big toxic trait in a relationship, which also comes under being cheated on. I have briefly explained online before that I have been cheated on, but I have never really found the words to describe what happened. Now that I have come to terms with it and I am moving on and learning from it, I think it is the right time to give everyone the lowdown and dissect the situation for you like I did mentally for so many months. Hopefully you will learn from it and be able to spot any similar behaviours in situations you are in, which may enable you to get out before it is too late.

The overlap

It all began a few years ago in December. I matched him on Hinge (are you even surprised at this point?). I remember when I matched him because it was on my mum's birthday, but as it was over Christmas, I didn't go back on the app for a few days to respond to his message. I didn't realise I hadn't responded to him for three days, but once we had been dating for a few months he often reminded me of this. Once I was back in Manchester after the festive period, we continued to talk but moved it over to Instagram DM, and after a few weeks he came over to mine for our 'first date'. This is the first mistake I made: we never went out of the house for our first date, which, granted, is not always a bad thing, but I have learnt now that a little effort to take me for a drink is not too much to ask. He only lived a two-minute walk away from me, which was very convenient, so a few days after our first date, he came over again, and this was when I realised which I liked something about him.

Liking someone is a big thing for me, and not something that comes easy. My friends always make a joke that I only ever see someone once and then I move on, which is true, but until then I'd just never taken a liking to someone enough to honestly want to see them again (despite me claiming to love everyone as soon as I meet them!). The second date went well, and things started moving in a good direction. The third time I saw him I went over to his house and met his housemate, and I really started enjoying spending time with them both. I think I liked it a lot because this was something so new for me, and I had never really allowed myself time to get to know a boy, so to finally do it felt good. From the third date, which was mid-January, all the way to March, things went from strength to strength (in my head) with him – every couple of nights we could go round to each other's houses and cook dinner, and the nights where we wouldn't see each other we would sit on FaceTime and play chess. I told him I loved chess, and apparently so did he, so the first time we exchanged numbers he sent me a chess game on iMessage, which I thought was sweet. Don't you love modern-day romance?

The only thing I thought was strange, and what started the doubts in my mind, was the fact that we never told each other verbally how we felt. I knew how I felt, and I like to believe deep down he knew too, but despite us sleeping together all the time, that was really the only form of affection he would give me. He'd always kiss me on the forehead goodbye, but I wondered why he never wanted to kiss me when we were just lying on the sofa, or when we were in bed. Maybe he just wasn't affectionate, or maybe he just didn't want to, who knows?

I say that was the only thing I thought was strange, but it wasn't. We also didn't go outside the house, on a proper date, for around two months. At the time, because truthfully I liked him so much, I let this slide, but it was always in the back of my mind. Finally, one day in March, he messaged and asked to take me for dinner that evening, and I remember you could not wipe the smile off my face for the entire day. I got home and got changed, and he took me to this cute Italian restaurant not far from where we both lived. He bought me a meal and then we went for a drink after, and he made a joke about taking me on holiday for my birthday, which was seven months away, so I started to think, okay, yeah, maybe he does like me after all. For the rest of March we went on a lot of cute dates. We went bowling, took the dogs to the beach, went on late-night Tesco trips and filled the car with snacks to go, then sat at different viewpoints of the city. It was really everything I had ever wanted, and I fully let my guard down for the first time in my life.

In April, I was going away for pretty much the entire month. I was first going to LA for work then flying straight to Florida for a trip to Disney with my family, so we weren't going to see each other for around four weeks. This made me very nervous, but if we could get through that I assumed we would come out stronger and maybe move things forward when I got home. I hoped he would ask me to be 'exclusive' or at least tell me he liked me before I went, but he didn't, which was another thing I thought was strange. The last night before I left he stayed round mine, and as he was drifting off to sleep he muttered 'love you'. I was facing the opposite way, and I also knew he was asleep, but I said 'what?' because I was in pure shock, and he said it again, 'love you'. I never told him he did this, so he might know, he might not, but I didn't say it back out of fear he didn't mean to say it. Looking back, I don't think I was ready to say it because I was always too scared it was going to end. Whilst I was away, he was booked in to have surgery with a lengthy recovery time, so we both knew things were going to change when I got home. But having that night together and him saying that to me, whether he meant it or not, meant a lot to me.

When I flew to Florida, he FaceTimed me the night I landed and spoke to my mum and little brother. He told me he missed me, and this was the first time he had ever said those words out loud, so I thought maybe I didn't have anything to worry about. Whilst I was away, his surgery was pushed back and he also went abroad, and every night he got in, even at 6am, he would call me to let me know he got back safe. All these little things he was doing on the surface made me think everything was okay, but I just couldn't help shake the feeling that it wasn't going to last, that something was wrong. I landed home, we picked up from where we left off and all was still well. As his surgery was still delayed, he asked me to come home with him for the night, back to his home town so he could show me around. He showed me the pub he used to work at, took me for dinner at a beautiful restaurant, and I met his parents. They were so lovely. The only offputting thing was as we were driving home, he told me meeting his parents wasn't a big thing as lots of girls had been back to his. I remember my heart sinking and that feeling of 'something is off here' came flooding back.

A few weeks later, he invited me back to his family home for the full weekend while his parents were away, so I drove down and spent the weekend with him, helping him recover. I was only meant to stay two nights, but on the morning I was supposed to leave, as his parents were coming home, he told me he didn't want me to go, so I stayed another night, and his mum cooked us all dinner. That night when we were in bed, and he asked me if I could be anywhere in the world right now, where would I want to be. I lay in silence for a few seconds and thought about it, but there was nowhere else I wanted to be. As cringey as it sounds, the only place I wanted to be was with him – we fell asleep in each other's arms, and this was probably my favourite night we spent together.

This is when everything started to go south. No more of the soppy stories, this is where we enter the zone of situation – where it became a situationship. Admitting this is horrible, as I haven't told anyone this apart from my mum, but driving back home from his that morning, I sobbed. I sobbed like a baby. My guard was gone, and I knew how much I liked him, but I just knew, my gut was telling me, that it was coming to an end. When he moved back to Manchester, we started to see each other less and his replies got slower. I found myself checking my phone every few minutes to see if he had responded – and this is when you know you're in deep. We did then go on a trip to London, but we started to argue. He would take out his frustration on me and say I was always too nice to him, but there is nothing wrong with being too nice. Weirdly, he then decided to speak about us, and for the first time told me he had deleted all his dating apps, he wasn't speaking to anyone else, and made us exclusive. We agreed to see no one else, were only sleeping with each other, and it felt good for a while, but he was putting in no effort despite doing this and I honestly thought enough was enough. I'm not ashamed to admit I wanted more – I wanted flowers, I wanted cute date nights, but most importantly I wanted to feel loved. And I didn't. I need to be told how someone is feeling, for them to be vulnerable with me and emotionally available and he just wasn't, so I made up my mind and decided I was going to end things.

Sometimes, no matter how much you like someone, you like yourself more, and removing myself from the situation was the healthiest thing to do for myself.

I went round his and told him my decision, and I was truthfully not expecting the reaction I got. He finally opened up to me. We cried, we laughed, we sat in silence, he understood my decision and told me it was a case of 'it's not an if we will be together, it's a when'. But it should never take it getting to this point for someone to tell you how they feel, they should tell you every day, and you should never have to question it. We agreed to be friends and when I left the next morning, he still messaged me, so I felt better knowing that even though it didn't work out romantically, I would always have him there as my best friend. This is where it goes even more south.

Four days after we called things off, he decided to tell me he'd found himself abroad for the weekend. The first strange thing about this was the week before he was claiming he couldn't even walk round to my house as the recovery was that bad, so to now be walking around a different country screamed fishy to me. I asked who he was with, and he would ignore the question every time I asked, so I just knew it was another girl. He still messaged me throughout the whole weekend, but I just couldn't help but think this was strange. I was flying to Greece on the Tuesday for a girls' holiday, and on the Monday night I had a call from him, which I didn't pick up, and when I asked the next day why he called, he claimed he wanted to see me before I went away as we would always see each other the night before I flew anywhere. I got on the plane and flew to Greece and tried to forget about everything – partying with my friends and meeting lots of new people was exactly what I needed. Towards the end of the holiday, me now being single, I decided to kiss a boy in a club. It was a drunken mistake, but it was funny, why not? The next day, I get a message from him (not the boy I kissed) and he said he hoped I had a good night with my boy last night. My jaw dropped and my brain started doing somersaults as to how he knew something had happened. He then told me he had seen it on a rep's story, because I was kissing in the background. I did not follow this rep, so he had done some digging to find this video. Now I did a stupid thing and lied, I said I wasn't kissing him in the video – we were just talking. But

I only lied because I still liked him, so much, and the thought of me upsetting him was a lot for me to bear. He obviously did not believe me, but when I landed home, we spoke on the phone for a few hours and cleared things up.

He was moving away for university around a month from this point and we still had a lot of each other's things, so a few weeks went by and we met up to give them back. We hadn't spoken in these two weeks, but he was watching everything I was doing as he even knew what colour dress I was wearing on a night out I went on that I never posted about, so I was confused as to how he even knew. I asked him if he was speaking to anyone, to which he responded, 'No one new.' New? So, you're speaking to someone you already know? Excellent. My whole energy changed, and I left not long after that; we hugged goodbye and that was that. I was so angry I planned to never speak to him again, not because that's what I wanted, but that's what he deserved. It had been a matter of weeks; you surely can't move on that quickly.

Fast-forward to August, I had him muted on everything to stop me from seeing what he was doing – I was in my healing era, okay? My mum asked me how I was doing, and it prompted me to check his socials for the first time. I clicked on his story, and there was a video of him and a girl on a boat on the river in his home town. I instantly just knew, this was her. It took me no longer than a few seconds to look on her profile, and see a picture of her in France, holding a rose, in the same place he had posted stories. She captioned the photo with something romantic, so I looked through her highlights. A few weeks after we had split it was apparently her birthday, and he had bought her presents, balloons, flowers, and laid them all out in his apartment for her, which she had posted. You would not post this if you had just been seeing someone for a few weeks, this had been going on for a while. A little further digging, and I found a video of her going to see Steven Bartlett in March, filmed from the exact same angle to which this boy had also filmed him from, when he went to see him in March. This night in March when he went to see him, he told me he was going out with a friend, I never questioned it as I had no reason to. Bull**** was it a friend.

It only took me a few minutes to sit and piece everything together. How long had this been going on? How could I have been so stupid? How did I not notice this before? My immediate response was to unfollow and block him on socials. I was so angry, hurt and upset, but more so disappointed. I felt disappointed in myself for letting someone like that into my life and letting them so close to me, but on the other hand I went with my heart and let myself feel, so I turned that disappointment straight back round on him as none of this was my fault. Around the time of this happening, there was a trend on TikTok outing boys for basically being not as nice as they seemed. This was so fitting for my situation so I made a TikTok about it, of course not naming him or revealing who it was. No one even knew I was dating him online, so only the few people I had told would have known who it was about.

A day later, I got a phone call from him. He was extremely disappointed in me, as this TikTok ruined things with him and his new girl – or should I say old girl. I laughed down the phone; the audacity for him to tell me I ruined things and now because of this she doesn't trust him. She should never have trusted him to begin with, none of this was my doing, he got caught out, and he was mad he got caught out. This phone call lasted several hours, as after he calmed down, he said I was the only person he wanted to speak to, and despite the anger I felt towards him I still sat there and spoke to him, because that soft spot for him didn't just disappear overnight. He said he felt weird talking to me about her, but honestly at this point I was past caring so I asked all the questions I wanted answers to. He told me when they went to France it was just friends – weird how there are pictures of him kissing her on the forehead on the balcony on social media, though, I don't do that with my friends. I said to him, you cheated; we were exclusive, and he was seeing another girl the whole time. He now claims she was his best friend; he'd never mentioned her to me before, despite having told me about all his other best friends. But now that makes sense because he never wanted me to find out. The funniest part of all is he could not say the word cheat. He used the word 'overlap'. He admitted that there was an overlap between me and her, wouldn't tell me for how long but I already knew so he didn't need to confirm that for me. He had been sleeping with her whilst sleeping with me too, so thank you for that one. We ended the phone call after a few hours and he said to me he didn't know if she was going to forgive him because of my TikTok. Funny how he thought my TikTok was the thing that had caused all the problems, not his actions over the past however many months. I wished him well and assumed that would be the last time we would ever speak. I was wrong; the story doesn't end here.

Two weeks passed of not speaking. Of course I was

still thinking about it, but never speaking to him again was the decision I made in my head, and I thought he'd made in his too. Until my phone rang and it was him. I answered, and he seemed fairly upset so I asked him what was wrong. He told me how his life was falling apart, nothing was going right with her, and he had spoken to the boys about it all but the only person he wanted to speak to was me, and that he needed to hear my voice. We spoke again, for hours, and he would always ask me for advice, he told me he liked the way I was always so positive about everything, so I calmed him down and told him everything was going to be okay. That was strong of me, looking back. Telling the boy I had been falling in love with that everything will work out with the girl he had cheated on me with. I guess the sad truth is I liked him so much that I wanted him to be happy, and whether that was with me or not I didn't care. Towards the end of the call, he asked me if I could not tell anyone he had called me, as if she found out it would come crashing down again, so I promised I wouldn't say a word. He told me we couldn't speak again as she didn't want us to be friends, so I said OKAY, and I never heard from him again.

This was a bittersweet moment for me. I finally felt that I had closure from the long ten months of an emotional rollercoaster, but the hardest part of it all was losing my best friend. I questioned everything for a few weeks, whether anything was ever real, what he even ever thought of me. I felt like I had lived a lie. I'll admit, I felt worthless. How did I go from being the happiest I had ever been to the saddest? Now looking back at the situation, it was all one big learning curve. You ask yourself, why? I now know how I deserve to be treated, what not to accept, when to stand up for myself. But most importantly, that it's okay to feel. Opening myself up to him and being vulnerable was something I didn't know I was capable of as I had never done that before, but to know I have the capacity to do that and will do that again is a beautiful thing. Everyone must experience sad times to appreciate the happy ones, and even though it took me a while, I came out the other side a changed person, stronger than before, thankful this had happened to me. He wasn't the person for me, he left my life at the time he was meant to, and who knows if our paths will ever cross again.

I'm still living in his head rent free, though. We both unfollowed each other from Instagram at the same time when all of this was going down. I was under the impression that when you unfollowed someone they would automatically be removed from your close friends' stories, however, I found out this was not the case. In April, nine months after we last spoke, I decided to upload something onto my close friends and guess what? He viewed it. Still stalking me nine months down the line? Stay unforgettable, girlies.

Writing that was almost like a form of therapy. I think I blocked out a lot of the good memories we had because they were so warped by the bad ones, but reliving those ten months in a short story wasn't as bad as I imagined it would be, and that's on growth.

Setting boundaries

One of the biggest lessons I have learnt from being in several toxic situations is that setting boundaries is an absolute *must* for me going forward. A lot of the time, if you go into a situation with no boundaries, no slight walls up, then the other person will immediately take the upper hand with an almost invisible hold over you, without you even realising you have given them this. This is where the power dynamic comes in. You often hear couples ask each other who wears the pants in their relationship, when truthfully, no one should, it should be 50/50. Each person has their own roles in the relationship but the feelings and respect for each other should be equal. A lot of the time, the only way for a man to understand this, unless he has been hurt in the past and understands this to begin with, is to leave him wanting more and to lay down the rules early on.

Here are a few boundaries that I think are important in a healthy relationship, or even in the dating stages.

Do not lie to me – An obvious one, but one that causes more problems than most. You should not have to make this clear to someone who wants to respect you, but it's always good to clarify so they know you are self-aware.

Respect my time – Everyone's time is precious, and it is not hard to stick to a time; for example, if you tell the other person when you will be meeting or coming home to them, etc. Of course, circumstances can occur that can affect this one, but if a man is asking you on a date at 7pm and not turning up until 9pm, he is not the one for you.

No lazy communication – This one is important. Communicating with each other is a key part of a relationship and the only way to build a deeper connection. If your partner is emotionally unavailable, or always avoids talking about the situation you are both in, you need to make it clear that this can't continue. From the very beginning make it known that you want clarity the whole way through the talking stage, all the way through the relationship and beyond. Once one person shuts off communication everything is bound to come to a halt, so lay this one out in the early stages.

Sexual boundaries – Again, one of the most important ones. Make your boundaries here crystal clear – what you like, what you don't like – and never go beyond what you don't like, even if your partner does like it. It is your body, and the person you're dating should respect that, just as much as you should respect their boundaries.

Values – This one might not be that obvious, but opposing views can cause problems. This is not to say your opinions can't differ, and opposites don't attract, because in a lot of cases they do and everyone loves a healthy debate, but, for example, if the boy you're dating thinks it's okay to be texting other girls whilst seeing you and you're not okay with it, then you need to set a barrier. Don't get too carried away with this one if your favourite colour is orange and his is green, I'm talking about the deeper things here.

When I am dating now, I will always ensure these boundaries are set before things start to get somewhat serious. A few of these, like lying, lack of communication and respecting my time have been glossed over by men I have dated in the past, leading to an outcome of us ending on bad terms. Setting boundaries is okay: you must protect yourself and your own feelings when going into a relationship.

The dreaded ick

A word we love to dish out regarding others but would hate to hear about ourselves. The ick. If you don't know what the ick is, a textbook definition would be:

> **Ick**
>
> This is a term for something that triggers a feeling of disgust or aversion towards something or someone.

Now, disgust is quite a strong word, I wouldn't say that when I get the ick I am necessarily disgusted, I am more politely put off. Nowadays, people's icks have gone above and beyond to the point where I laugh at some of them and think how can that even be true? A few of my favourite ones I have come across are:

The backpack – Am I going to be shallow and admit this is one of mine? Slightly. I don't even know why because a backpack is practical and what else are they meant to carry their things around in? But something about it sends shivers down my spine. I think what makes it worse is when you take the thought of them with a backpack on even further and imagine them running for a train, or being late for the bus, and the backpack jumping up and down with them as they are running. It's just a funny thought in my head, and I know this is quite a common one.

Being rude to a waiter – Yes, this gives me the ick. I don't think it takes a lot to be polite to a waiter or a member of the public, so when someone is rude to them, it's an instant no for me. If they can be so rude to someone they don't know, it makes me wonder how rude they are to people they do know, and I just think it's bad manners.

The baby voice – I think this one is a split 50/50 love or hate for a lot of people. I have never done this with anyone because the thought of it honestly upsets me. I have had boys speak to me in the past in a baby voice and it's an instant turn-off for me. If you do this and you don't get the ick then I am very happy for you, because I wish I could find it cute.

Pet names – Again, like the baby voice. I know so many of my friends have pet names for their boyfriends, but I just can't get with it. Cuddly bear, sweetie pie, baby cakes, stink. It's not happening for me, I'm sorry.

Naked in a bath – This wins the award for the silliest ick of them all but by far the funniest. Imagine the boy you're seeing sitting naked in the bath, rocking back and forth in shallow water. Who even created this one, because why would your boyfriend rock back and forth in a 5cm deep bath? But no matter how much I loved someone, the thought of them doing this makes me laugh out loud.

Now I was intrigued, what do icks look like for a boy? I decided to ask in a few of my group chats for some of my male friends' icks, and here's what I got back . . .

Boy 1 – Girls wearing the wrong shade of foundation, smoking and loud chewing.

I was pleasantly surprised by these, as they are more general and less far-fetched than a lot of the ones us girls tend to come up with. I hugely agree with the loud chewing one, this aggravates me so much and if a boy was to do this early into seeing me, I think I would also pick up on this. My friend also said he thinks icks are silly. He claims it annoys him because a lot of the things are so random, and his top example was when a girl gets the ick because a boy is using an umbrella. Something so practical yet it's seen as an ick. It doesn't make sense.

Boy 2 – My other friend said he doesn't have any, which I found quite refreshing to hear.

Nowadays I think the word ick is chucked around too easily, so to know that from a boy's perspective he can't think of any makes us girls feel a little better. He did say he hates the ick that girls have when a guy must move the car seat forward to reach the pedals. This one made me giggle, but I get where my friend is coming from, not everyone is over six foot. We must appreciate our short kings too.

Then I sent the same question into my girls' group chat, and I was howling at some of the responses.

Jasmine – When the boy must retell the joke because no one heard it the first time and they didn't get the laughs they were after.

A tame one to begin with, but I was howling at the thought of this.

Sophie – When they are dancing to the beat drop of the song but going too early. Also, having sharp toenails.

I'm agreeing with you on this one, long toenails are not a vibe.

Flossie – Choking on a yoghurt, not fitting in the bath, choking on water and it is spilling down their chin, standing at a buffet, slipping pool side, the robot dance, and the worm, getting lyrics wrong on their own, asking for something on the menu and it's not available, eating fish fingers, a bath with no bubbles and standing up and the chair tipping up.

I opened the group chat to Flossie sending this extensive list and I have been in fits of laughter ever since. What made it funnier was this list was written on her notes and she screenshot it, but it was last edited in 2022, meaning this girl has a permanent list of icks on her phone. The fish finger one got me; what on earth is wrong with fish fingers?

These are a real mixture of mild to severe ones, some realistic and some very unrealistic, but the real thing to think about is why do we honestly get the ick? A lot of the time, I think we are seeking excuses to leave, so we look for every minor problem to be used an excuse, like the backpack. Someone owning a backpack is not a reason to not want to date them, it is in fact an excuse.

When I came out of my situationship, I quite quickly went into dating other people, but would look for every ick, aka excuse, for them to not be the right person. Maybe this was because I was trying to fill the void of the person I had just lost, and no one was matching the connection I had previously formed so I was purposely giving myself the ick. There was one boy I was dating for a while, who I really liked, and now nearly a year on I wish I could message him again but I most definitely could not out of embarrassment. We'd known of each other for a while and when I moved to Manchester, he asked me on a few dates. I didn't say yes for few years – yes, a few years – but when I became single again, I thought why not? We were in similar industries so we got along well and I thought he was beautiful... always had done to be honest. We were dating for a month or so and then one evening we were both out, so he came round to mine for an after party. This was the first time he was going to be staying over so I was excited. We got into bed and the first thing that went wrong was he chucked my teddy onto the floor and laughed at me for having one. Now, yes, he probably got the ick with me for having a teddy, but don't chuck it on the floor please. Then we get undressed and I see two tattoos. One of his ex's names along his chest, and another of his ex's initial on his foot. I asked a few of my friends if I was in the right here for getting the ick, and some agreed, some didn't. TMI, but how am I meant to have sex with you whilst staring at your ex's name? Impossible.

It gets worse because things slowly fizzled out between us, and I really did not think he listened to my podcast, *Sex, Lies & DM Slides* with my best friend Saffron, so I explained this story on the podcast. A few months later, he bumped into all my friends in a bar and told them how his sister and ex had both listened to the podcast and clicked it was about him. He said there were no hard feelings and reflecting on the situation in a much more powerful headspace than I was last year, I could have got over it and am still tempted to message him sometimes, however I don't blame him if he never wanted to speak to me again.

This is a prime example of forcing yourself to get the ick. Instead of doing this, I don't think it's a bad thing to admit you just aren't interested or aren't ready within yourself to move forward with someone. Forcing yourself to get the ick is much harder than being honest, and I have recognised that in myself now.

One thing I do believe in, however, is when you truly like or love someone, the ick does not exist. I have been in love twice in my life and liked a few people deeply, and when I would picture any of those people running with a backpack on down the street, naked in the bath or calling me sweetie pie, I didn't get the ick, because I didn't want to. This further backs my point of the ick being an excuse, so as a matured version of myself, we are renaming the ick, and if I am ever in a situation with a boy where I find myself looking for an excuse, I will simply be honest and leave. The dating process is a learning process; no one is going to get it right the first time, or the second time, or probably the third, but that is the fun of it. We are experiencing all different types of men, learning as we go.

RECOGNITION

Recognising that the ick is technically an excuse is part of maturing in the dating world, but another part of understanding the ins and outs of it all is recognising red flags within ourselves. A common occurrence for me in my dating life would be self-sabotaging relationships. When I look deeper into why I do this, it's kind of sad. I have been treated very badly by certain boys in the past, I have never really felt like I was someone's number one priority – apart from my recent ex-boyfriend, who you will hear about later, but I could never enjoy this because my past trauma from boys well and truly took over. Due to the treatment I have received, it almost plants an invisible seed in your mind that every boy is the same and is going to treat you the same. So even if I really like someone and they have done nothing wrong, shown no red flags, I will somehow find a way to sabotage the situation by forcing myself into believing something is wrong. I either make up a red flag, telling myself they are messaging other girls or, if I am really struggling for a way out, imagine them naked in the bath, rocking back and forth.

I hate the fact that I do this, but I look at it as a form of self-protection. I know how hurt I have been in the past and I know that I don't want to feel like that again, so I self-sabotage to prevent it happening. What I need to stop doing is telling myself something is most definitely going to go wrong. How do I know that? I know from past situations that I love hard. Once I decide that this person is my person, I will put everything I have into a relationship, and I love the fact I have the emotional capability to do that. But if I never give anyone a chance, how will I ever get to this stage again? I enter every situation now with caution and I won't give my all straight away so I can protect my energy, and this way I know my energy is going to the correct people. Never feel guilty for looking out for yourself; just make sure you can decipher the line in your own dating life between protecting your feelings and sabotaging a good situation.

This was a heavy chapter to write – coming to terms with the fact I am slightly toxic, self-sabotaging my own situations and forcing the ick upon myself. But like I said, self-recognition is the first step to becoming the best version of you. I smiled to myself when writing that, but at least I'm smiling at my own writing and not some silly boy's message I have been waiting on – we love growth.

Chapter 4

Being Single

OH, THE JOYS. In the last three months, I have become single again. I broke up with my boyfriend and re-entered the dating world. You're probably reading this thinking, boyfriend? If any of you know me from oversharing my life on social media, you would know I never really posted my ex anywhere online, but I did say I was in a relationship. I suppose to make sure you're following along, I need to give you the lowdown on my ex.

We met on Hinge. You could have written that part of the story for me at this point, because that is where I meet every boy ever. We matched a few months after I came out of the 'overlap', so it was quite soon, but at the time I thought I was ready to get back out there. We went on a date and, honestly, it was one of the best first dates I have ever been on. We went to play The Cube and then spoke for hours in a bar afterwards. I knew there was something different about him as we bonded over a lot of similar topics and he just seemed different to the rest. We went on two dates, but then I went backpacking around Australia. I had told him I was going to do this when we first met so when it happened it didn't come as a surprise, but still, to have gone on a few dates with someone and then go off to travel the world for six weeks kind of throws a spanner in the works.

The time zones made it difficult to talk all the time, and I was, of course, still technically single, so whilst I was away travelling I did have my fun, which I think he always knew I was going to do anyway. Having only been on two dates I was doing nothing wrong at all. When I got back from Australia, we saw each other again and I guess this is where it truly started. I could tell for the first time that I was his number one priority, and that there was no one else on the scene, but my self-sabotaging personality would constantly tell me I wasn't good enough to finally receive this treatment from someone. We had a lot of fun with each other, and one of my favourite nights was a date in the Northern Quarter; we were meant to only go for a few drinks and three hours later I was drunk, in his office, playing strip ping pong. You can laugh at me all you want but it was hilarious and very much a turn-on. In February, he took me on my first proper Valentine's date, and one thing I love about this story is that Valentine's, which was around five months after we first started speaking, was the first time I slept with him.

There is absolutely nothing wrong with sleeping with someone the first time you meet them, or the second or the third, but after everything that had previously happened to me, I was adamant on building a much deeper, emotional connection with someone so that when the time did come to further the connection, it felt different. Without going into too much detail, yes, it was worth the wait. Fast-forward a few weeks, and we were sat in Roxy Ballroom in Manchester of all places, and we told each other we loved each other. I knew how badly I wanted to say it, but I wanted him to say it first, and he did. Knowing I was in love with him was something I was okay with; I knew he would never hurt me. Sometimes with certain people you just know;

I never believed people when they said that, but it is true. In March, he met my mum. I had never introduced anyone to my mum before, so this was a huge step forward in the right direction for me. My mum loved him – I still remember the look in her eyes when she looked at us both together. She has known how long I had wanted a man like him, and the sparkle in her eye was that instant approval for me, that he possibly was the one. After he had met my mum, he then asked me to be his girlfriend. No big, romantic gestures, just simply us, lying in bed, thinking about nothing else because nothing else mattered in the moments we both shared, and it was official. I had a boyfriend! I never thought I would see the day.

Everything was good for a while, but if I am being completely honest, I was just too busy for a relationship, and I don't think I was truly as happy as I wanted to be. I think this was because I had always imagined what it would feel like to be in a relationship, and for me, it didn't feel like I thought it was going to. I am a very independent person, so letting my guard down to allow someone in, no matter how much I wanted to, really was not as easy as it seemed, and I slowly started to distance myself from my own boyfriend, which makes no sense – it should have been the opposite way round.

I decided to make the horrendous decision to break up with him and, yes, it was horrendous. I had found someone who treated me with every ounce of respect I have always wanted and deserved. He never did a thing wrong, he loved me unconditionally and I so wish I was able to love him back the way he wanted to be loved, but I sadly could not. So that brings us to the current day. Single, and back out dating. I just have to say, he is, and forever will be, one of the best, most patient, loving people I have ever had the pleasure of loving, and I am so happy that through everything we are still good friends.

You're probably also thinking, why would I be dating if I have just said I don't have the time for a relationship, or I couldn't let my guard down with him? I understand, I guess it doesn't really make sense. But now removing myself from the situation and essentially dissecting it, I have realised that as hard as it is, maybe he wasn't the one for me. Someone can give you everything and more, but that does not mean you have to stay with them if you aren't happy. Maybe I am too used to toxic men that when a nice guy comes along, I run. It is sad because I was very emotionally ready for a relationship during my situationship the previous year, but he was not emotionally available. Due to this, I then became emotionally unavailable myself and met someone who wasn't. It was one big vicious cycle. Maybe I'll regret my decision in months to come, but it's a decision I have made for now. Who knows what the future holds? As it stands, I am back out enjoying my single life, ready for the next adventure my heart is going to be taken on.

So now you know the back story of my ex, let's talk about being single. I think there are so many amazing reasons to enjoy being single, some of which are...

No more waiting for the message ... When you really like someone, it's quite common to constantly check your phone to see if they have replied. When you're single, you aren't waiting around for anyone to message you! You can go out with your friends and enjoy the evening with your phone in your bag. A dream.

Freedom to focus on yourself ... Coming out of a relationship often means you need some 'you time'. Now you are single, you can have all the you time in the world. Endless pamper nights, movie nights, the bed to yourself. But most importantly, time to fall back in love with your own company.

Time for a new hobby . . . It's the cliché one, I know. If there is something you have always wanted to do but never had the time whilst dating, you can now do it. Join that dance class, go and learn how to cook, or start reading a book. Doing something new is an amazing way to spend your single time.

You can flirt with whoever you want . . . I love a flirt, so this was one of my favourite things about becoming single again. When you're out with your friends and you see a cute boy at the bar, just go and flirt with him, what have you got to lose? No one's saying you need to take them home with you at the end of the night, but a little bit of harmless chat doesn't go amiss.

It's YOUR time . . . Falling back in love with your own company is one of the hardest things to do when you lose someone – and if you have never been in a relationship before but absolutely love your own company, that is exactly what I want to hear. Being comfortable enough to stay in, cook dinner, light a candle and watch a movie all alone without your head running spirals is an incredibly hard thing to do, but once you master it, you open the doors to a whole new level of peace, power and strength. Nothing is more satisfying than being okay in your own company and thoughts, so being single is the perfect time to work on this.

It all begins within

One thing I have learnt from being single is that it all begins within, and the value we hold within ourselves. I sat myself down and really thought, why do I find it hard to be in a relationship? What is the problem with me? It's not a problem, but there is a deeper-rooted reason.

When I was growing up, I never knew my dad, and I still don't know my dad. He left my mum when she was pregnant with me and ran off with another woman to have three more children. I grew up with a stepdad, who was incredible for the nine years I got to spend with him, but he and my mum then divorced when I was ten, so our relationship past that has remained over text and I haven't seen him for over five years. My nan has been single for my entire life and has never dated since I was born, and so has my uncle, so I have never been surrounded by a healthy relationship in my family. This almost doesn't sound believable, and it was a real glitch-in-the-matrix sort of situation, but I was at Disneyland with some friends a few years back, and I saw my dad with his three children. I knew what he looked like as I had done some digging on Facebook. Seeing him in real life, with three other children who he loved unconditionally, hurt. I felt like I wasn't good enough – why would he love them and not me? Now I am older, I know it has nothing to do with me, he never had the pleasure of growing up with me and seeing me blossom into the beautiful young woman I am now, so more fool him. But I think children in these situations tend to go one of two ways; they either crave the love from a significant other so bad they hop from relationship to relationship and despise being single, or they are extremely independent to the point they find it impossible to let someone in because they fear going through the hurt all the people around them did. I am safely option two. Coming to terms with the fact that this is a big reason why I am the way I am has been hard, because I one day dream of being married, walking down the aisle in a beautiful white dress, starting a family, but my brain also doesn't realise that in order to have those things I need to be okay with letting someone in. And yes, love is scary, it's one of the most terrifying, vulnerable life experiences a person can go through, but it can be beautiful, and it will be beautiful when my time to have this comes.

    The first step in any situation is acknowledging

where you are going wrong or why you are the way you are, so by recognising this in myself, I can now take the necessary steps to help myself open up, and maybe, just maybe, trust a man again. I think through all of this, I have truly become so comfortable in my own company, and I am learning to love myself again. I love nothing more than coming home on my own, giving myself a nice pamper and cooking myself dinner, because I want to give myself all the love before I begin giving love to someone else. A few years ago, this was not the case and I used to look for value for myself within men. I would feel upset if I wore something nice and the guy I was seeing didn't compliment me. I'm embarrassed to admit that it would sometimes affect my entire night because it would make me feel like I wasn't good enough. This probably stemmed from when I was seeing a boy for nearly a year and he complimented me once in 11 months. But the truth is, you don't need a man telling you that you look good; if *you* feel good, that is all that matters. If a guy thinks you look good, that is a bonus.

These are a few of my favourite ways to learn to love yourself, without the help of a man.

Stop comparing – The number one thing we love to do is compare – compare ourselves, our lives, our relationships to someone else's. This is a major downfall for all of us. We are all beautiful in our own individual ways and just because someone else has something that you crave, it doesn't make you any less of a person inside. Stop comparing yourself to others and, instead, remind yourself of your 'past you' and look at how much you have grown.

Learn to let go – Learning to let go and move on from past relationships and past mistakes is not as easy as it sounds; it takes a lot of time, effort, determination and personal growth. Learning to move on from situations is okay, and even if the reason isn't quite clear for the breakup in the current moment, the time will come, and everything will fall perfectly into place.

It's okay to say no – I used to be such a yes person, I would say yes to everyone and every event because I didn't want to miss out or say no, but part of loving yourself is only doing things that you really want to do. I think that's a big part of growing up and if you don't want to do everything your friends do, that is okay. Saying no is normal, and no one should make you feel bad if you just want to do something for yourself.

Accept that some people won't like you – This is a bit of a deeper one, but we might as well get straight to the point. Just like you don't like some people, some people also might not like you, but that does not mean there is anything wrong with you, it just means it was not meant to be with that person. It's so easy to experience rejection and then turn the reason they rejected you into a newfound insecurity, but instead, love yourself for what they didn't and when the time is right, the right person will love you for everything that you are.

Write yourself a love letter – Practising self-love might seem a little daunting at first, but there is no better way to do it than writing a love letter to yourself. There are so many reasons you should love being you, so express them! Whether that's physical features you like about yourself, or qualities you love, let yourself know you are happy and proud of the person you are, and express all the positive things you think about yourself.

The pressure from society

Dating in our generation comes with a lot of pressure, much of which originates from everyone's online presence on social media. Social media can be seen as something incredible, but also petrifying. I found a way to use social media to build myself a career, connect with new friends and all of you reading this book, and essentially build a brand. However, social media within dating has unleashed a whole new world of expectations, which is scary. Even for me, who knows that the social media world is ultimately not real (despite everyone doing such an incredible job of making it appear so), it has led me to believe relationships should be a certain way and I should be at a different stage of life to where I am now – all because I have seen a few people on social media doing something I 'should' be doing.

Social media has warped everyone's expectations of what a perfect relationship is. For example, Kylie Jenner, who is only a few years older than me, has posted hundreds of pictures of her house being filled with the most beautiful flowers from her various boyfriends, which is amazing, but not an everyday occurrence for most people. Travis Barker created a full rose garden consisting of millions of beautiful red flowers on a gorgeous beach to propose to Kourtney Kardashian. Another example, a little more common but still one that I am yet to experience: the rose petals on the bed. Not quite as extravagant as millions of roses, but still the same gist. Now yes, I do want to experience this. Every time I see people post this on their story I am so excited for them, but seeing all of these things gives you expectations of what you want a man to give you in a relationship. That's perfectly fine, as you are allowed *as many* expectations as you want, but it can lead to the downfalls of relationships because if your boyfriend doesn't do big gestures like this, but someone on your Instagram feed does, you might think, *Well, he doesn't love me, he's not doing this for me.* The reality is that might not be his love language, and he can love you unconditionally without putting rose petals on your bed or filling your living room with one million roses. A lot of the time, people are only going to post the highlights of their relationships on social media, they aren't going to livestream an argument, are they? My point is, social media is a highlight reel of someone's life, and a lot of the time, it isn't all as it seems online, so comparing yourself to what you are seeing on your Instagram feed is never a good idea for anyone.

Another pressure that has grown from social media in relationships is that you always feel like you are behind someone else in your life. When I was younger, I thought I would be in a relationship by now with someone I was potentially wanting to marry and start a family with. I always envisioned myself engaged at 25 and now I am getting close to that, I am so far away from this happening, and that is okay. Society puts a lot of pressure on relationships, saying you should be doing this by a certain age, and you should be engaged by the time you are 26, when that is not the case for everyone, and everyone does these things in their own time. Each person's pathway is different, and that is what makes life so beautiful, and so unpredictable.

I will admit, there have been so many times, at the age of 23, where I have felt like time is running out, and for me to even have those thoughts is crazy. I always thought I would need to be with my person now so I could be with them for a certain number of years before we get married and buy a house, but that isn't the way my life is working out, and I have slowly become okay with that. I do get lonely sometimes, especially because two of my best friends are in relationships, so I occasionally have sat back and looked at them and thought, yeah, I want that. It's hard when your friends are in relationships and you are not even close, and it does make you question is there something wrong with me, why has it not happened for me yet? The truth is my time hasn't come for me to meet my person, but when it does, it will all make sense.

Ultimately, as hard as it is to ignore, there is no need

to feel pressure from society to jump into a relationship just because it feels like everyone around you, and everyone on social media, is. Rushing into something just to fit in is never going to end well, and learning to accept that it will happen for me when it happens is another step forward in the right direction for me to fully love myself, and also for me to have a healthy, happy relationship in the future.

Healthy relationships blossom when both people are ready for the relationship and all the work that comes with it. Relationships should be fun, flirty, effortless and full of love, but of course they take work and effort, too. When you are fully happy within yourself, putting effort into a relationship will come naturally because that person will be enhancing your life, adding to what you already have, not filling in the gaps that you feel need to be filled with a partner's presence.

Valentine's Day

Okay, so it's 14 February. A day that everyone in relationships looks forward to, and a day that all of us single people dread. There is so much pressure about Valentine's Day on social media; you see red roses everywhere, surprise holidays, beautiful meals out – it honestly feels like I have seen every surprise ever being given to someone on this day.

As a single girl, I have a love/hate relationship with Valentine's Day. I have also experienced some of the best Valentine's dates and the worst, so it would only be right to share these and make you feel better about spending your Valentine's Day alone, if you are.

THE PERFECT DATE

I briefly touched on this when speaking about my ex-boyfriend, but he made Valentine's truly special for me when we were together. He pre-booked my favourite restaurant a month in advance – I had mentioned it to him when we first met and he remembered. I got all dressed up in a beautiful black dress, he wore a suit, and he knocked on my door with a big bouquet of red roses. It was honestly the most perfect night. I surprised him on Valentine's morning before he went to work and dropped off his favourite dessert – a box of shortbread – outside his house with a cute love letter. I love cringe stuff, I'm sorry.

'THEY ARE TOO EXPENSIVE'

This was my Valentine's experience from the previous year when I was seeing my situationship. We had been seeing each other for nearly two months, so I wasn't expecting anything huge, but I was excited as we had spoken about Valentine's and doing a few different things, so I was hoping for a surprise. It got to the day... and nothing. I was picking up my new car that day, so that was a present to myself, and later that evening when I went to pick him up in it, he was passenger princess instead of me. We never ended up going for dinner, or doing anything like that, instead we decided to go and do a food shop. Fine, practical, at least I am ticking something off my to-do list. But then, we get to the shop, and the first thing we see are hundreds of bouquets of Valentine's flowers. Beautiful red roses, some big bunches, some small. We walk over to the flowers, and he picked up one of the bunches, I remember my heart racing with excitement because I had never been bought flowers on Valentine's before, and instead of him putting them in the trolley, he put them back, walked off, and said they were too expensive. These flowers were in the sale, for no more than £4.00 as it was 9pm on Valentine's evening, and he couldn't even buy me them. I know he wasn't hard up for money, so it wasn't that. It did hurt. It's not about the money: if he genuinely couldn't afford the flowers I would have been okay with it, but he knew I had never celebrated a Valentine's in a good way with a boy before, which is why it hurt more.

THE BREAKUP

I can't quite believe I experienced this on Valentine's – literally the opposite to what the day is meant to be about. I had met this boy at a festival the previous year, and we had been speaking for a few months. I went round his house and met his mum, we FaceTimed every night, and I genuinely at the time thought he was going to be my boyfriend. It was a few days before 14 February, and I was in the supermarket with my two best friends, Haz and Byron, shopping for drinks, food and presents for the boys we were seeing. Can I just add this was the same shop as the previous story, so clearly me and this shop don't go hand in hand when it comes to Valentine's! I bought a few bottles of wine, a Valentine's Day card and some chocolates as he was coming up to spend the weekend with me, and I was excited as I thought this was going to be the first time I celebrated Valentine's with a boy. Yet again, I was wrong.

It got to the Friday morning when he was meant to be arriving, and I heard nothing. I called, no response.

I double texted, still no response. Until later that evening when he started typing a message to me and was typing for what felt like hours. I opened the message and it was him telling me that we were finished, and he wasn't coming to stay with me for the weekend. No explanation, it just ended like that. The sweetest part of all this, however, was Byron saw how upset I was over this situation, so he wrote me a Valentine's card and put it in my letter box for me to open. At the time, he signed it anonymously, so I didn't know who it was from, and this cheered me up when I was sad. I later found out it was him and he told me he did it because he didn't want my Valentine's ruined because of a silly boy. Of course, I had an idea that there was a further explanation as to why I got dumped, and a few weeks later I found out he was seeing another girl, as they decided to go Instagram official. History loves to repeat itself, as this has happened to me twice now. They say everything comes in threes, but hopefully it will be third time lucky for me.

I have had a varied range of Valentine's experiences, as you can tell, but my favourite way to spend the day is with my girls for *Galentine's*.

> **Galentine** – a beautiful, funny, intelligent and wonderful person. Someone who is there for you through thick and thin, no matter what. The person you can call anytime about anything. The one who will keep your secrets close, and who you can trust with your life. The best friend a person could ask for.

I have spent more 14 February dates with the girls than I have a boy, and I am seriously okay with that. I don't think the day needs to be just about romantic love, I think it can be celebrated in all relationships, such as family and friendships. There is nothing better than getting all your friends together and using it as an excuse to go out, get drunk and party all night.

> ### Saffron's take
>
> I've embraced Galentine's for many years and had some fun evenings with the girls watching films and having a laugh together. We all love a good romantic comedy where we can gush over our celebrity crushes, but I have always looked

> forward to spending it with a man and being in love! I think Galentine's is super fun with your girls, but obviously it will never be as romantic and I'm a true romantic at heart! I do love when my boyfriend surprises me for Valentine's Day with a cute little spa trip or some flowers being delivered to the house. I believe every day you should show love to your partner, but I look for any excuse to show it a little more and Valentine's is the perfect time to do that.
>
> *Saffron Barker*

If you are wanting to spend Galentine's with your friends, here are a few ideas for things you could do . . .

Exes-themed cocktail night – I don't know if you have seen this trend on TikTok, but it is one of my favourite ways to get lost for hours. Themed cocktail nights are always fun, and basing them on your ex on Galentine's just seems very fitting. One by one you each bring out a tray of cocktails connected to your ex, such as a cheetah cocktail if they cheated on you, a red drink with a flag in it if they were a walking red flag, a tiny COCKtail (if you know what I mean), a fishbowl, a sharing cocktail if they were a man of the town, or a hazardous-themed drink if they were toxic. I feel like the list here is endless and you can really have some fun with this to make each other laugh.

Wholesome painting evening – Another popular trend on TikTok, but getting all your friends together for an artistic evening is an amazing way to express some emotions and creativity. You can each have a blank canvas and some paints and create whatever you feel like while sharing a bottle of wine. I love seeing what people come up with when they do nights like this, and you could even add a theme if you wanted, such as destinations, flowers or naked life drawing.

Go on a road trip – Why does Galantine's have to be just one day? You can make a whole weekend out of it! Grab some drinks and board games, pack the car and get out of town. A little lodge with a hot tub would be perfect for an occasion like this, not to mention all the lovely meals you can cook!

Baking evening – Baking your favourite dessert with your friends is always a perfect way to spend your evening.

You could even make a Galentine's-themed spread and make everything pink and red. Or, make mini cakes, and each sit and decorate one! I love the trend on TikTok where you write a quote on a simple heart-shaped cake – this would make for a very cute photo too.

Bring a board night – Quite like the exes cocktail-themed evening, but this time with food. Allocate each of your friends a dish to contribute so one person brings a charcuterie board, another brings a dessert platter, another a main, and have an evening indulging in good food. Sticking with a colour theme is always fun, so everything could be pink!

A Galentine's gift swap – I have done this with my best friend Saffron before, and we filmed it for YouTube. You set a budget, so for example £50, and buy the other person some of their favourite things. It's funny to add in a few Valentine's-themed presents, such as a 'Grow Yourself a Boyfriend' toy or a pack of condoms, just some funny gifts to make the other person laugh in their single era.

Friendships in life are everything. I am blessed to have some of the most incredible people around me, and I wouldn't change them for the world. And friends are who you need the most when you're going through a breakup or trying to heal.

I have had to go through the 'healing girl era' a few times in my life before, but one stands out to me the most as my friends went out of their way, massively, to ensure I was okay. The last day I saw this boy, we had to swap back all our things that we had from each other's houses, and we had one of each other's books. One of my favourite books is *Happy Sexy Millionaire* by Steven Bartlett, and weirdly it was also one of his favourites, but he had annotated his and I had annotated mine, so we swapped books and re-read them so we could see what each other had written on the pages, and how we had each perceived what had been written. When we switched our books back, the last thing I wanted to do was keep my book. When you're in a relationship, I think some people can be okay with keeping physical memories of their ex or someone they were seeing, but others prefer to get rid so there are not constant reminders of that person around. In that moment, I wanted rid.

This wasn't an easy thing for me to do as I had spent hours annotating that book, but it needed to go. My friends took me out to a lovely canalside pub, we had a few drinks, and they told me to bring the book with me. As we were walking home, they took me onto a bridge, and I closed my eyes and screamed everything I hated about this boy, and why I was better off without him, then you can probably guess what I did. I chucked that book, as hard as I could, into the river. As I was watching it drop, I almost felt like time had just frozen, my heart was beating one million miles an hour and my brain went all fuzzy. It was one of those moments where you are almost physically saying goodbye to an old chapter of your life and opening a new one. My friends all cheered and when I came out of the brain fog, I started laughing and almost shed a tear. It was a significant moment for me because my friends recognised the hurt I was experiencing and tried to turn that round into a moment of humour to make me feel better, and it really did.

Just to clarify, we did not leave the book in the river. One of my friends waited for it to float to the side, picked it up, and put it in a recycling bin. My mum then bought me another copy for Christmas that year, and I re-annotated it in a whole new light.

Friends truly are for ever, and in the darkest time I am so glad they tried everything they could to bring a little smile back to my face. Steven now has a new book, so let's hope my next boyfriend doesn't like it too, because I'm not throwing this one into a river.

Diary Entry

Still very single, still not enjoying the dating experience as much as I had hoped. I matched a boy on Hinge several months ago now, and we went on two dates. One for dinner, where we ordered a lot of food that we never ended up really touching because we were too nervous to eat in front of each other, and another where he came over and bought me my favourite McFlurry from McDonald's, which was sweet. I enjoyed spending time with him, but I got busy, and we were struggling to find time to see each other. I then went on holiday on a cruise and the first night you get on the ship, there is a sail-away party where everyone goes up to the top deck for free prosecco. Now they say everything happens for a reason, and it truly does, because this is weird. Two people came over and introduced themselves to me, saying that they live in the same building as one of my best friends, and then asked if I know this boy. The boy who I had been on two dates with. I said yes, and they proceed to tell me how they randomly met him at a festival, where he was showing strangers my photos, asking them if he thinks I am a catfish. Why on earth would you show random people my photos? I think it's bizarre. One of them then asked me if I was still seeing him. I had not replied to his latest message for a few days because I had been so busy, so I said not really. Well, it was a good job that was my answer. He then proceeds to tell me that he was meant to go to the gym on Friday with this boy, but he had cancelled on him as he was sleeping with a girl that evening instead. Now of course, when you're dating, it's normal to date several people at once, but this was just more information than I ever needed to know, especially when I had just come away on holiday. So that was the end of that. I am glad I found out because I didn't really get a good feeling about him anyway, but I just thought what a small world, and what a way for me to find out. So now I am single again, talking to no one. I love my single life.

Except a few days after writing this diary entry, the plot thickened. Remember my situationship from Chapter 3? Well, we had not spoken in over a year, no contact, apart from him viewing my Instagram stories, which I guess isn't even contact, that's just regret. I was lying in bed watching a show on my laptop – it's gone midnight at this point – and my phone rings. Guess who? HIM. The way I gasped I wish I had my reaction on camera. The funniest part about this whole thing is that that week I had two people that I used to speak to crop up and message me; one from when I was 19 and one from when I was 20. They both asked if we could meet up as we were overdue a catch up. So original – I love it. When the second boy messaged me, Freya, one of my best friends, was round my house and I read it out to her and joked 'it always comes in threes, who is going to be next?', then four hours later, this. I honestly sat there and thought this surely must be a mistake. About 15 minutes after the call, I texted him and asked if he meant to call me, and an hour later, just gone 1am, he replied: 'I did.' Just that: 'I did.' What sort of context am I meant to get from that?

So I responded and asked if everything was okay. The following morning, he sent me a message explaining how one of his friends from work was moving into my building and they had a 'chaos emergency', so because I live in the building, he thought I could help. At 1am. Originally, not one part of me believed this as it just seemed very random, and so out of the blue, however, I have spoken to him further and he explained what happened to me, so maybe this was just his way of trying to reconnect. So strange, but you know what they say, they ALWAYS come back. No one watches you closer than the people who have done you wrong.

Overall, being single clearly has its challenges, and that's okay, but it's also the perfect excuse to invest time in myself and spend more time with my friends and loved ones. I hope that I come out of this stage of my life a stronger person, having learnt more about myself and what I am like on my own, so I know what I can be like in a relationship. Also, I want to have put more love into myself and ensure that I know I *AM* worth it, and have spent the first half of my twenties with some of my best friends, making memories to last a lifetime. I truly do feel so content and happy to be single at 23, it feels extremely good to be putting myself first.

Chapter 5

Entering into a Relationship

ENTERING A RELATIONSHIP is, for the majority, a very exciting time. You will be falling in love with someone and enjoying every minute. However, it is not always plain sailing, and there are often a few tricky areas to navigate to get that perfect relationship and to live happily ever after.

When entering a relationship, everyone loves to talk about the infamous stages. I think they differ from person to person, but this is what I have experienced and tend to run by.

THE SINGLE STAGE

This is where you are dating different people and figuring out which one could be the perfect match for you. You have no loyalties to anyone at this stage and no one has any loyalties to you, as this hasn't yet been discussed; you're simply enjoying meeting new people and having some fun.

THE TALKING STAGE

You have met someone and you are texting them daily. This is when it starts to turn fun and flirty, and you really get to know them on a deeper level. I love and hate this stage because on the one hand it's so exciting when you get that little butterfly feeling inside, because you know you like someone and texting them every day grows that feeling even more, but then when you start to get REAL deep into this stage and you begin smiling at your phone, you're in trouble. I feel like this stage can also contain a few games and headf***s. Boys think it's fun sometimes to be on their phone at that moment, but to not respond to your message and instead post an Instagram story. I personally don't understand this; if you're on your phone, reply to the message, and if you're not, just reply whenever you get the chance. Playing games and doubling the time they took to reply for you to respond is only going to end up in someone getting hurt. In this stage, you could technically be texting a few people at once. I find it quite hard to do this just in case I get the conversations mixed up, and because I prefer concentrating on one person at a time, but at this point you haven't normally discussed anything hugely deep, so you're still safe to be exploring your options.

EXCLUSIVE

Oh, the lovely exclusive stage. Sometimes this can be skipped and you'll go straight from talking to someone to being in a relationship with them, but nowadays this is an added stage because we all find it hard to trust in our twenties, apparently. Exclusive means you are only talking to and dating that one person, and you have both agreed this. It is a nice feeling as it is a step forward in the right direction; however, you don't want to get too comfortable and sit pretty in this stage for too long, as it feels like a cop out in some ways.

THE RELATIONSHIP

You have made it through all three stages and are now entering the relationship stage. You're now official and have completed it all. You will probably be in the honeymoon phase – this isn't a stage, more a few months where you are completely and utterly obsessed with each other and live in a cute little bubble. This phase could fade out for some people, and for others it could last the entirety of a relationship, but either way, it's an exciting phase to be in, especially when you're in love.

Now we have clarified what the four different stages are, let's discuss timings. I have a personal preference on this now after going through different timelines with different boys, and of course every relationship is going to be different, but these would be my rough timeline boundaries for my future boyfriend.

Talking stage: 2 months
Exclusive: 2–3 months
Relationship: 3–4 months: 4 months max.

The reason I say no more than two months in the talking stage is because you know if you see something going somewhere with someone after a month. I have been in a talking stage with someone for six months, and you never know where you stand. I ended up really liking him by the end of that time, but we had no exclusivity, so even though I was not seeing anyone else, he could have been, and I would not have been able to say a thing about it. Being in the talking stage for a lengthy amount of time is a cop out, it's a way to keep someone there if you're bored one night and want a bit of fun, or keeping them there as an option if your first choice falls through. This translates back to setting boundaries: don't let a guy mess you around and keep you waiting.

But do you even think we should have stages? Part of me does, because I think it gives clarity to the other person, so you always know where you stand. Imagine if you were talking to someone and also speaking to a few other people at the same time because you didn't know if they were also doing the same thing, then you turn up for a date and they ask you to be their girlfriend or boyfriend, what do you do? But then on the other hand, like I said before, are stages just a cop out? If you are in them individually for a respectable amount of time, I think stages are necessary, but anything over my suggested timeline could possibly be a red flag.

Dating with an online presence

Just as a little background information, I have shared my life on social media for over ten years with people, which, considering I am only 23, is quite crazy to comprehend. I have always wanted to keep my dating life quite private, as I have seen a lot of my friends in this industry post their relationships, and it can become one of the reasons that they sadly end up breaking up. Because of my privacy in this area, I think when I do decide to post something like a soft launch, people are a little more invested as it is something I don't naturally share, so they are a little nosier. The idea of my future relationships being private, but not secret, sits well with me, but of course it all depends on how much my partner would want me to share, so a lot of factors come into it.

I have found it very hard to date due to my job, because boys think with their dick half of the time and message me some beautiful one-liners like these from Hinge:

Boy #1 – 'Is this going to feature on your podcast?'

This has become an increasingly popular one, which does make me giggle because in the early stages of me getting these messages, yes, it probably would have featured, but too many boys have tried this one now that it doesn't really work, so maybe we need a bit more originality.

Boy #2 – 'Hello, you'

This one honestly makes me laugh every time because I have joked online about how when I used to slide into a guy's DMs, I would always say, 'hello, you'. I think I would always put this because I struggled with knowing what else to say, and the 'you' adds a slightly flirty hint to the message. I have joked about this so much on my podcast and in my YouTube videos, so a lot of boys will slide in with this now. It went so far that this quote was on a billboard in Leicester Square with my face on, so as funny as it is, maybe leave that one to me, boys.

Boy #3 – 'Didn't you used to date . . . ?'

When I was 16, I made a few YouTube videos with a huge British YouTuber, who I do not fancy naming because the regret is real. Those videos BLEW up, but because he had a more male-based audience, I started to get a lot of guys come up to me once we ended, and even seven years later, I still get people asking if it was me. Yes, it was me, but for bringing that up, you have ruined your chance.

I think the other thing about dating with an online presence is that it makes it hard to see what people's true intentions are, and whether they like you for you, or like you for the numbers you have on socials. I have got better at figuring this out in the early stages, as it is obvious if they genuinely have no idea who you are, or if they have seen you on socials before. I am not opposed to dating someone who has seen some of my content or heard my name floating around, I just would not want to date someone who aspires to being in the job I am in, and sees me as a lead into the industry. Yes, it could work out perfectly and we be together forever, but if it doesn't, I have a public breakup on my hands and he got exactly what he wanted.

Saffron's take

Dating in the public eye has always been an interesting one. I have tried to not let it affect my dating life, but of course, sometimes it can. My previous relationships have all been shared online, so in a way people see this as an invitation to comment on myself and my boyfriend. It isn't, but because I share all my life online, it would be hard spending so much time with a boyfriend and not posting them and sharing it with everyone. I recently did a bit of a wild hard launch with my boyfriend because I just thought, why not? We did a collaboration post on Instagram, so it shared onto both of our feeds, and I think it is safe to say that no one was expecting it, so reading everyone's reactions and positive comments was so lovely. I know Anastasia has never hard launched a boyfriend, and her attempts at soft launches have not always worked in her favour, but when the time does come where she has a partner who she wants to share online, I will hopefully be the person she comes to for some advice and I can guide her through it all.

Saffron Barker

Do I think dating with an online presence has hindered me? Maybe slightly, but that is just because I am more aware of sharing things. There was one boy I dated a few years ago, that we found out afterwards was genuinely just in it for the clout. Get this . . .

This is the blind-date boy I was writing about a few chapters ago. We got on well at first, ended up dating for a while, like I said, but then the plot really thickened. I found out a few things I wasn't fond of about him, so I decided to end things. A few weeks later, he meets my friend, who is also an influencer, and begins dating her. Just to add, his girlfriend before dating me was also an influencer. There is a common theme here, isn't there? My friend and I found out after we both dated him that he'd stated he wants to date only influencers or models who have a lot of money (he had daddy's money, but we won't go into detail about that), so he wanted someone to be able to essentially keep up with him. Everyone is allowed a type and to be as picky as they want, but this made me question whether he was dating me for me or because I fit the job description. This is one experience that made me a lot more wary with dating whilst I am growing my online platform, to say the least.

POSTING YOUR PARTNER ONLINE

This is a conversation that is a must when dating in your twenties, because it is beyond rare to find someone now who does not have some form of social media. When wanting to share a relationship online, I think every single person is going to have different opinions of when you should post, or whether they want to post their partner at all. Some people smother their Instagram feeds in images of their partner, which I think is lovely if that is what makes them happy, but other people will just post the odd story, which I also think is lovely. Posting your relationship on Instagram is the new Facebook relationship status; when I was 13 and dating in secondary school, the most exciting part of it was getting to change your relationship status on Facebook, as it would get the whole class talking.

So, if your partner says he wants to post a photo of you both, when is the right time to do it? I don't think there is really a right time, but I would wait until you are officially in a relationship to do so. In the talking stage I personally would not post a photo of him, just in case everything dramatically changes the following week. But once you are in a relationship, I think this would be the right time to post your partner, if that is something you both agreed too. Another little touch I love about posting your partner is having a highlight dedicated to them, or all the things you both do together on your profile. I have seen a few boys do this and I think it is so sweet, as it's not plastering them everywhere and making their personal account a couple's fan page, but instead posting the highlights and good times of their relationship all in one place. If you're going to do this, once you have posted who it is, you can then go and add into the highlight all the soft launch stories you had previously done, so it's like a little story of you both on your Instagram profile. I've seen some boys name the highlight after their girlfriend, or I have seen some just simply use a heart emoji. Either way, I think it's a nice way of showing you're in a relationship with someone.

One thing I cannot stand, however, is when people put their partner's name in their Instagram bio. We are no longer living in 2012 when BBM was all we lived, breathed and slept and would put all our friends' names in our names, just to show them how much we cared. I think if you're putting your partner's name in your bio, that is coming from a place of insecurity because you need everyone to know you are together, and they are yours.

Is it better to do a grid post, or do you prefer stories?

A grid post is always there on your profile, whereas a story is going to disappear after 24 hours, so I personally would opt more towards a grid post, if you are 100 per cent sure you want to go Instagram official. It is a little harder for me: if I was to have a boyfriend now I don't think I would opt to do a grid post as soon as we become official, for reasons that I have previously explained, but if I wasn't in a job where thousands of people were going to judge what I post, I would definitely go straight for the grid. But then if you want to delve even further into this, do you do just one post dedicated to them, or are you posting a photo of you both mixed in with a photo dump, where they are not in the photo that will appear on your grid? One of my best friends was in a relationship with someone last year, and she posted him quite a few times on her Instagram feed, bearing in mind she is also an influencer so was getting a lot of attention on her relationship-themed posts. However, her boyfriend would never post her on a grid post, and the one time he did, it was in a carousel photo dump where she wasn't visible straight away on his profile. A few months after, she found out he cheated on her by finding messages between him and a different girl. I think the reason some boys do this is because when a girl clicks on their Instagram and has the first initial scroll, unless they are going straight in for the full-blown stalk, if they can't instantly see a girl on his feed they will assume he is single, therefore he will gain a follower and probably a DM slide. My best friend brought this up to her boyfriend, and he must live in a different world to us, as he claimed he didn't want to post her on his main grid as he was going to gain more followers without her on it, which would help his modelling career. I can't . . .

However, it's a tricky one, because what if your boyfriend is completely and utterly in love with you, but he just does not want to post on social media because it is not his thing? This is very possible, as I have been on a few dates in the past where I have asked them if they use social media a lot and they really don't. They will have it, but they post on it once every few years, maybe even less. It's hard in this day and age to comprehend that someone might not need to post you and show you off on social media to know that they love you, because we are so conditioned into thinking everything needs to be shared. It is, of course, lovely to be shown off on socials by your partner, but if your other half doesn't want to be shared, try not to jump to conclusions and think the worst. I have been deeply in love with people in the past and never shared more than a hand at a dinner table. Love is NOT defined by how much you post for others to see, it is defined by how much you give each other.

The soft launch

A soft launch is honestly one of my favourite things EVER. I love when people I follow on socials post a picture at a dinner table, where it's obvious they are on a date, but you can't see who with. Or when people post a photo of a bouquet of flowers, or a hand hold. It's basically a treasure hunt to try to find the person down their following and have a little stalk, and I can guarantee every single person has done this at some point in their life because we are all so nosey.

If you are wanting to soft launch your partner on your socials and make it very extra, here are a few ways you could do it . . .

Hand hold – Whose is the mysterious hand? This is most definitely giving away the fact that you are with someone in a romantic way, but not quite ready to share who they are.

The hand on a steering wheel – If your partner is driving you around, why not take a photo of their car, or their hands on the wheel, or their hand on your leg whilst you are passenger princess? Another good way to let people subtly know you are taken.

The mirror photo – This would take some time to take, but why not take a photo with you in it, with them facing the other way, or them hugging you from behind so the phone covers their face? I like this one because I think it's a cute photo to have on your phone as a screensaver, but also a good way of showing people who they are without seeing their actual face.

Soft launches, however, can go very wrong, as I have learnt from experience. I have done a few in my time, and here are some of my most memorable.

The dinner table – This was with my situationship last year. At this point, we had been seeing each other for a few months so I thought it would be an appropriate time to post a little teaser on my story. I had been doing this for a lot longer than people probably realised, though, as I would post pictures of the beach and the dogs, where I would be with him, but people never knew, or cute nights in my apartment where he would be there, but the one that really did it was the dinner table. We had gone out for dinner in his home town, and we both took a photo of the food on the table, from different angles originally. When we got back to his later that evening, he was getting quite a few messages from people saying that they had seen us out, they were wondering why he was with me, why I was in this town, etc., but he brushed them all off. That night, I posted a picture on my story of the dinner table and I think I put a heart emoji or something similar on the picture to insinuate it was a date. I had a few people reply things such as 'Soft launch?!!!??' 'Is this your boyfriend???' 'Who are you out for dinner with?' but of course I never replied. The following morning, we were lying in bed, and he decided to post the photo of the dinner table, but he posted the same one as me, and within two or three hours, my DMs were flooded. Someone must have gone down my following to find him, then watched his story and pieced it together, or someone he followed that also happened to follow me figured it out, and that was it. To be honest, because I was serious about him, it didn't overly bother me because, granted, I didn't want people to start to follow him or anything, but if people knew we were dating I didn't see that as a bad thing. He, however, deleted the story as soon as people started to message him asking if he was out for dinner with me. I remember thinking at the time, I wonder why he's deleted it, and of course now we know it was because he was seeing another girl at the same time as me, so that would have thrown a real spanner in the works for him.

That was my first case of a soft launch going wrong. With that in mind, moving onto soft-launching my actual boyfriend earlier this year, it went even worse.

The tattooed arm – Soft-launching my ex-boyfriend was something I was admittedly nervous about because of what had gone wrong the previous year for me. When we went on dates, I would never post a thing and I kept it completely private. I was enjoying that, and so was he, as he is a naturally very private person. One night we went on a date night, and we came back and climbed into bed with a huge McDonald's order – I mean, standard night out routine, if you ask me! I took a photo of the food, and in the photo was his arm, and he has a sleeve tattoo, so that is a clue for people who were trying to find him because they could just match up the tattoos. So, I posted this photo the following morning, but after about 15 minutes I decided to delete it. I was getting flooded with messages saying they could now find my boyfriend and I didn't like the idea of that, more so because he didn't want to be posted everywhere or shared online at that stage, so I was looking out for him when deleting it. I should have learnt from previous experiences, but this won't happen again.

Then, a few nights later, he was round mine and we were having a games evening playing Monopoly, a lovely wholesome date night idea, and suddenly out of nowhere his phone was blowing up with hundreds of Instagram follow requests. I instantly knew in my head that someone had found him, and must have posted it somewhere. We decided to try not to let it ruin our date night, until his brother called him because he had been sent a TikTok of him that someone had made, with all his old LinkedIn photos, his old workplace photos, and wrote his Instagram username on the video. I instantly panicked because I choose to put myself out there, so the photos I post online I am prepared for people to comment on and pick apart if they feel the need, whereas he, someone who is super private, had never experienced anything like this before, and as many lovely comments as there were, there were also a few bad ones. It mostly just consisted of people tagging their friends and responding 'omg this is her boyfriend' but still, it wasn't ideal. Luckily, he has promised me that he will never go public on Instagram, and therefore no more of his photos can ever be posted anywhere and no one can see if he posts a story, etc. It was a lot at the time, but I can only thank him for being so incredibly amazing about it, because some people would not take their privacy being tampered with very lightly.

However, don't let my experiences with soft launching put you off, I think this has only gone dramatically wrong for me in both instances because of my whole life being online.

Let's meet the family

Meeting the family and friends is, in my opinion, a very big step forward in building your relationship with someone. I think it's easier if you introduce them to your friends first and then your family, as I can trust my friends to tell me honestly before I go through all the effort of introducing them to my mum. I've introduced two different people to my friends in the past, and one to my mum. I think meeting my mum is a huge thing, hence why I have only introduced my mum to my ex-boyfriend, but I have met several people's parents and friends, and had some interesting encounters.

As I said in the last chapter, when my ex-boyfriend

met my mum, it really was something special. I was so scared to introduce him to her because I had no idea how she was going to react, what questions she was going to ask, and in all honesty, how she was going to be seeing me sat there with a boy. It was something she had never done before, and even though I have always told her everything about my dating life – and by everything, I mean *everything* – she had never seen me in a fully happy, comfortable situation, so this one just felt a little different. We met in London and went for lunch, and like I said, the sparkle in her eye when she looked at us both was everything I needed to know without her even saying a word. She did ask what his intentions were with me, and as soon as that question came out of her mouth I wanted to shrivel into a hole and not come out because I didn't want him to feel like it was a game of 21 questions and he was being put on the spot. But his answer was beautiful and everything a mother would want to hear from someone who is dating her daughter. I remember we said goodbye to her, and she sent me a text message straight away saying how much she liked him, and he told me how tight she hugged him once they had spoken. It really was that seal of approval that I needed. I never actually met his mum, due to us not being together officially for that long, however, it was something that he always spoke about, and if in the future we were to ever rekindle, it would be something that would happen very quickly. I spoke to his brother briefly on the phone, and he always told me his family were constantly asking how I was, so it was lovely to know they cared and even though I never met them, I felt extremely welcome in their family.

When I was in a situationship, I did the opposite. I met his parents, but he never met my mum. As I wrote when explaining the situation between us, he told me that meeting his parents was never a big deal, due to how many girls he had brought to his home previously. However, when we spoke things out a few months later, he said to me he did realise he had said this and said to his friend when I had left that he'd made it out to not be a big deal, and she'd told him this was a stupid thing to do. When I went back to his family home the second time, I was only meant to stay for two nights but ended up staying for three, and his mum and dad came back on the third night from their weekend away and cooked dinner for us. We spent several hours downstairs chatting and had a glass of prosecco, and it was lovely. When he asked me to stay this extra night, I did say, 'But your parents are coming back,' and he didn't mind. I think he was subtly trying to make up for what he had said the first time, to make me feel a little more welcome and less like 'just another girl'.

This is the big difference between meeting someone's parents when you are in a relationship versus meeting someone's parents when you don't know where you stand with each other. When I introduced my ex to my mum, I was introducing him as someone I saw a future with, therefore I feel like there was a little pressure deep down because it was a big moment, whereas when I met my situationship's parents, there was no introducing me as his girlfriend or girl he was speaking to, it was technically just him introducing me as a friend.

I have also met the parents of another person I was speaking to – the boy who called it quits with me on Valentine's Day. As we lived a few hours away from each other, when we saw each other, we would meet in the middle and go for a date in London, or it would have to be round one of our houses. He invited me over to his house, and I ended up meeting his mum and his brother. Again, as we were just in the talking stage, he didn't really introduce me as anyone, just a friend, but his mum and brother were lovely, and we all sat and had dinner together.

This kind of situation is one of those where it's awkward; I'm excited to meet a boy's parents because in my head that's a good sign that they want me to meet them, but both times I have done this when we haven't clarified what we are between ourselves and it has never worked out. If someone were to ask me to meet their parents now before I knew where we stood, I don't think I would do it, purely because I want to know that I am meeting someone's parents as someone who is potentially joining the family, not just as a friend.

Saffron is arguably better placed to comment on meeting the parents than me because she has had a few more positive experiences...

Saffron's take

My parents told me to never go somewhere empty handed! So I think a small gesture can often go a long way, for example, a bottle of wine, flowers, etc. It doesn't need to be anything big, it just shows you've put some thought in, and they will be very appreciative. Weirdly, I was speaking to Anastasia about this the other day, as I recently met my boyfriend's parents, and she was asking me what I was taking and if I was nervous. If you are yourself and try to get to know them and speak to them, they will love you! If you are nervous, it will help to go prepared with a few questions – nothing crazy but, for example, what do you do for work, what's your favourite food, have you been on any holidays recently? If you are going round to your partner's house for food and their parents are cooking, you can always offer to help or see if there is something you can do. Little gestures go a long way and will be the start of, hopefully, a great relationship between you all.

Some other general tips:

- Be genuine and polite, show authentic interest in their parents and getting to know them.
- Be confident but humble, find balance between confidence and humility to make a positive impression.
- Show gratitude, if you meet them at their house, they have you over, etc., thank them for having you and hosting you.
- Find common ground; ask your partner beforehand about their interests so you can

> make conversation and see if you have shared interests.
> - Avoid any controversial topics, keep the atmosphere nice and light!
> - Give them a nice greeting, either a handshake or a hug – but I'm always a hugger!
>
> *Saffron Barker*

Meeting friends

Meeting friends is a little more of a laidback, funny experience. Is it better to introduce your partner to your friends one by one, or in a group situation? I have done a little bit of both, so I feel like I know what I prefer now.

When I was in the talking stage with someone a few years ago, I knew I wanted him to meet my friends so I could get their opinion on him, as my friendship group has VERY strong opinions on each other's partners and wants the best for everyone, so if there is a red flag, you best know it's being held against them by my friends. With this in mind, I decided to invite him to come for a few drinks with us all at a local bar, nothing crazy, but I thought it would be better to introduce them all together in a busier sort of setting, so hopefully he would feel less awkward, and there would be more conversations he could join in on rather than a one-on-one encounter. He came and we played a few drinking games, and my friends liked him. Of course, he was a little nervous, but he did well and off the back of this, my friends started inviting him to their parties, they would message each other in reply to each other's Instagram stories, the lot.

I think I did the right thing by introducing them all at once. When I met his friends, it was a bit of a random one. He had a flatmate so when I went round his for the first time, I met him straight away. We had dinner all together and watched *The Undateables* – of course we watched a dating show. This did feel a lot at the time, as I had only met the boy I was seeing twice, but his flatmate was lovely and by the end of it I classed him as a friend. I was in Ibiza for a work shoot, and it turned out his flatmate was also in Ibiza in the same hotel. We went for drinks just me and his flatmates' friends in the hotel, and it was nice to be that comfortable with his friends. They even all came back to where my friends and I were staying for an after's. Again, it was nice doing it in a bigger setting as his friends also met my friends that night, and it started a good friendship between us all. The funniest thing about this, though, was I never met his best friend as he didn't live in Manchester, but once we had finished and weren't really on talking terms, we bumped into each other in a queue for a bar one night and he was with him. His best friend didn't even say hello to me and instead looked the other way. How sweet.

But when it came to my friends meeting my ex-boyfriend, I went about this a little differently. The first time he met any of my friends was when he met Haz and her now boyfriend, and we went on a double date. We went for drinks and got SO drunk, but it was nice doing this in a date setting as the boys had a lot to speak about and I also had my best friend there with me to run off to the bathroom and get excited with. To meet all my other friends, we went out for one of their birthdays to do an all-day bar crawl dressed up as fictional characters, so again, very laid back, but the best way to do it. Everyone got along so well, and he got to bond with everyone without too much pressure. It was dreamy.

Another time I introduced someone to my friends was in a different double-date situation. I went on a double date with Byron and his ex-partner, and we went for a roast dinner. In my head, it was a good idea, but honestly, it was just awkward. It was one of those ones where the conversation was very surface level, and the boy I was seeing was just very egotistical, and to be honest, rude, so the chat was just dry.

So, what are the best things you can do when introducing your partner to your friends? Here is some of my advice . . .

On a night out, but bars only . . . The reason I say bars only, or pubs, is because you want to be able to speak. If you're introducing them in the middle of a club with pounding music, what is the point? You're not going to be able to have a conversation and you'll probably be too drunk to even realise you met them. Doing it in a bar whilst having a few drinks means you're in a social setting, which already takes away some of the pressure, and you can play games like never have I ever, so you can get to know each other a little better.

Give them the heads up . . . When you know it is time you want to introduce them, don't just spring it upon them a few minutes before. It's always better to speak to them about it first, to see if it is also something they want, then this gives you the chance to see how they would feel comfortable doing it, as some people may prefer a one-on-one encounter rather than a big social situation.

Wait at least three dates . . . The reason I say this is because you don't want to be in the situation I was in, and just meeting friends or parents because you must, you should be doing it because both of you want this to happen. I say three dates, but really I think it should be a few more, but on the other hand, I think you know after the third date if someone is just your friend, or if you see something more with them. So if you're wanting the guy you're seeing to meet one or a few of your friends after the third date, that's okay, just no earlier.

What do I wear?

Choosing an outfit for meeting the friends and parents is a lot. You want to make a good impression, but most importantly you want to feel good and confident within your outfit choice to be able to enjoy the experience. There's nothing worse than not feeling your best when you're on a date, let alone when you're meeting people who mean a lot to them. So here is what I would wear if I was to find myself in one of these situations again . . .

Trousers and a 'nice top' – I think this is everyone's go-to, but what does it really mean? Jeans are always a good idea, as these can be dressed up but also dressed down, and teaming them with a nice pair of trainers and dressier top (not a long, baggy one, maybe one that has a little more detail) is perfect.

A co-ord – This is a dressier option, but I think this always comes across as being very put together, yet effortless. You can get some stronger co-ords, such as a suit style, which I would probably avoid as those can be seen as a little professional, but a nice skirt and top one, or long trousers and a crop top could work perfectly here.

What YOU feel most comfortable in – It's all well and good me telling you what to wear, but everyone feels their most confident in all different types of outfits. What I would feel my best self in, someone else might not, therefore I think it is important that you wear something that you truly love, and feel the most YOU in. Yes, it is lovely to dress up, and first impressions are everything, but if you are going to feel 100 per cent yourself in jogging bottoms and a top, you wear that. It is what is on the inside that truly counts, so you wear your best self and, as cringe as it may sound, a smile! This is always enough and their friends and family, and them, will love you because you are being unapologetically you.

He hasn't introduced me to his friends . . . what does it mean?

The hard thing with this is that everyone is going to go about these situations differently. Some boys might want to introduce you to their friends straight away, whereas others might be a little more reserved and want to make sure you are 'the one' before they do so. If you have been dating for six weeks and meeting their friends hasn't even been mentioned, I think it's a slight warning sign. I know I would want at least one of my friends to meet the person I am dating by that point so I can see what they think of them, but I do know boys tend to think a little differently to girls.

Bottom line is, try not to panic. If you feel like it is getting to the stage of wanting to meet his friends, test the waters. Throw it into the conversation to gauge his reaction as to how he feels about the situation. If he has a positive reaction and agrees, you know you're on the same wavelength, but if he tries to ignore what you've said or not follow up on it, take this as a sign to maybe withdraw slightly, to prevent yourself from getting hurt in the future. It's very easy to assume that he doesn't want to introduce you to his friends because he is seeing another girl, or multiple girls, and is not sure which girl he wants himself, but this isn't always the case. If, however, he has met all of your friends and still hasn't mentioned you meeting any of his, I would take this as a slight warning sign – you don't want to involve him in things you're doing with your friends if he isn't doing the same in return.

What if I don't get on with his family and friends?

Firstly, why didn't you get on with them? Are they not your sort of people? Was the conversation dry? Did they not put in any effort to sit and speak to you? Figure out why you maybe did not get along with them, to see if it is something that can be rectified. However, for me, it is *SO* important that my partner gets along with my friends. My friendship group is what I class as my second family at this point, so if even one of them didn't like the person I was dating, if it was for a valid reason, it would make me reconsider the whole situation.

When you don't get on with your partner's friends or family, the first thing to do is speak to your partner about it. Get their take on it, and see why this might be happening or if it is something that can be worked on. It's not an ideal situation to be in, but nothing good ever comes easy.

Diary Entry

The last few weeks have been a little wild in my dating life, but purely because I saw my ex-boyfriend. Like I have said, we have remained good friends, so I knew it wouldn't be awkward or weird to see him in person, but of course I was nervous as we hadn't properly spoken in person since we broke up. The day I saw him, I was disgustingly hungover, so we were going to go for a walk, but my legs could not deal with that, so we went and sat outside for some fresh air. It was lovely, I'm so glad that above all I have remained friends with him and can still see him when I want to catch up. He has asked to see me again before I go away, so I need to figure out what is going on and how I feel about the situation, because seeing each other a lot, or multiple times over a few weeks, could potentially get a little confusing for both of us.

Chapter 6

Relationships that Go the Distance

RELATIONSHIPS CAN COME in all different forms. You can have relationships with your significant other, long-distance relationships, friends with benefits, situationships, the list is endless – but let's touch on one that we've yet to really cover: the long-distance relationship.

Can they really work? Or is it a recipe for disaster? I have never been in a long-distance relationship, or what

I would class as one anyway. The furthest someone has been from me who I have dated is probably just over an hour, but I'd consider long distance to be four to five hours plus, or where one of you is living in a different country. I do, however, have a best friend who knows *all about* these sorts of relationships as that is all she has ever really known, and potentially has a little kink for, so maybe it's best she tells you a little bit about them.

Saffron's take

It's not that I prefer them, I'm just not against them. All my relationships have happened to be long distance; maybe I just attract men that live further from me. Doing the job that I do, long-distance relationships tend to fit in to my schedule more and because I am used to them, I may just naturally attract that sort of relationship now by subconsciously wanting it. I just think distance makes the heart grow fonder! I'm very optimistic, so distance in my eyes will never be a problem; if it's meant to be it will be and distance won't matter.

While long-distance relationships can be challenging, they can also offer unique aspects to a relationship like:

- Personal growth – Both of you can grow individually, pursuing personal goals and experiences, which can contribute to a more fulfilling relationship when you're together.
- Trust building – Overcoming the challenges of distance needs trust and commitment, which can strengthen relationships as well!
- Quality time together – When you do get to spend time together, it tends to be intentional and meaningful and means you make more of an effort.
- Increased appreciation – Absence can make the heart grow fonder; being apart may lead to a deeper appreciation for each other and the time you spend together.

Saffron Barker

I do understand why Saffron likes long distance; with our busy schedules and constant travelling, it almost makes it easier to set aside a certain period to spend with someone, instead of just coming home after work and getting to see them all the time. It gives you time to miss them, get excited about seeing them again, and live your own separate lives for a little while. But then I also see how this wouldn't be to everyone's taste, as some people would prefer to come back from work and be with their partner and see them all the time. I wouldn't be opposed to a long-distance relationship, however, dating someone who lives in Australia, for example, I think would be too much. That wouldn't be as simple as driving a few hours down the road to see someone for the weekend, and time zones make even just talking to each other impossible. But you know what they say, if they wanted to, they would, and if it truly was the right person, distance or time zones would not stop you from trying to make the relationship work.

Saffron and I always joke about the fact that our dating lives have pretty much been the opposite to each other. Living in Manchester and predominantly using dating apps to find partners, it's quite easy to match with people who live within a one-mile radius. I could literally see into the apartments of my ex-boyfriend and the two guys I have had the longest talking stage with from different windows in my flat, and I kind of liked that. Whereas with Saffron, all her boyfriends have been further away than five hours in a car, and if she's going to date, she's dating abroad. Last summer we did a lot of travelling; we spent a month in LA, Palm Springs and Vegas to kick things off, then did a few days in Sicily, then headed to Ibiza for Saffron's birthday, then did a European cruise. I know what you're thinking, it seems a little excessive, but it was our first hot girl summer where we were both single and not seeing anyone at the exact same time, so we had to take advantage of this moment and make the most of it whilst we could. In two out of four of these holidays, Saffron decided to go on a date; one of them lives an 11-hour flight away and the other a four-hour flight away, so exactly what she was looking for. Nothing came from either of them, but I wish I had the confidence to go on a date with someone whilst I am on holiday. She met one of them on a dating app, and one of them in a club, yet on two out of four of these holidays, I ended up kissing two much older men, who I have never spoken to again. I would have preferred to have been in Saffron's position...

I don't think I would be opposed to dating someone who lives far away, or even in a different country, I just think that doing this comes with a few worries and concerns, but I guess some pros too. Let's dissect them.

Can a long-distance relationship really work?
Yes, it can, because . . .

You will most definitely have your independence – Being long distance means you won't be seeing each other every single day, and you will be living separate lives when you are apart. I think this is a good thing, as having your independence in a relationship enables a healthy outcome and healthy relationship to blossom. Being able to do simple things like your own food shop, going out with your own friends, little things like this, will stop you losing your independence within a relationship, which can sometimes be easily lost when you are spending every single day together.

You will be giving *ORGANISED* – If a long-distance relationship is going to work, this requires a lot of time, effort and organisation from both sides, meaning you're going to be very on top of your schedule. Organising times to call, weekends to see each other, it's really giving structure, and if you like structure, like me, this is most definitely a pro for you.

You build a stronger *emotional* connection – As you won't be with your partner as much as other people and won't be touching them every day or having sex every day, your emotional connection is likely to spike, as this is what you will be relying on to keep the spark flying in between visits. This is a good thing, as the stronger the emotional connection is, the better the relationship is going to grow to be.

It gives you time to miss them – I really like this one, as I know some people prefer to be with their partner 24/7, which is completely fine, but I think it's nice when you get a chance to really miss that person, so when you see each other again, you truly appreciate it. This will be a common occurrence in long-distance relationships, and you will probably sit and count down the days until you get to see them again. This will keep the passion in the relationship alive too, if you know what I mean.

It allows you to travel and see new places – Wherever your partner lives, it is different to the same four walls you wake up to every day, so it is an exciting thing to be able to travel and see them. Especially if your partner lives abroad, as there will be so many interesting things to do and see, and when they come and visit you, they will be seeing all of your usual sights for the first time, making it just that little bit more exciting.

But there are also reasons that a long-distance relationship can't work as well as you'd think.

It can't work, because...

You might struggle with loneliness – It's not something shameful to admit, as we can all feel lonely sometimes. If you are the type of person who loves to be around people all the time, a long-distance relationship would make life harder for you. It's fun because when you see them, you'll spend several days with them at a time, but when you head home to work for the week, the feeling of being alone creeps back in around 5pm as the laptop gets shut, and you want your partner by your side as you cook your dinner.

They might be tempted to cheat to fill a void – With you not being there all the time, they may be tempted to cheat because they want to have sex and you are several hours away, unable to partake. There is NO excuse for someone to ever cheat and if they do this and turn around and say it was because they missed you, I call bull****. No one should be tempted by anyone else other than their partner, no matter how far away you live from each other.

You might start to struggle with insecurity – If you are away from your partner a lot, you're not going to know what they are doing, and where they are a lot of the time, which might make you feel uneasy, and potentially insecure. Of course, you don't need to tell your significant other your every move, but if your partner hasn't told you what they have done for the last few days and you are suspicious, it can be a downward spiral from here. Which leads us onto the next point . . .

You can develop MAJOR trust issues – For this sort of relationship to work, you must have trust. You must trust each other with your whole heart, and not have a doubt, as this is where your situation could begin to suffer. This can take a big toll on your mental and physical health if you are constantly worrying about what your partner is doing, where they are, who they are with, so you must be prepared to often experience a little doubt at some points. I think it would be deemed normal to have a little doubt if you are committing to long distance.

You won't be having as much sex – This one might not be an issue for some of you, but this could be a massive issue to others. It all depends on your love language, and how high your sex drive is, but being away from your partner for potentially months at a time, not being able to have sex with each other and connect on that physical level, may take a toll on one or both of you. Sex in a relationship plays a huge role in deepening your connection with each other, so this needs to be taken into consideration.

There are as many pros as there are cons for long-distance relationships, and I truly think it depends on the individual, and their love language, as to whether it can work or not. Ultimately, if you want it enough it can work, it just takes a lot of commitment, and you must be prepared for a few hurdles along the way.

Situationships

Not quite a relationship, but a bit more than a friendship. I'm sure most of us have found ourselves in a situationship of some sort during our dating experiences.

By definition, a situationship is less than a relationship but more than a casual encounter or booty call; it refers to a romantic relationship that is, and remains, undefined.

I have spoken about one I was in a few years back, and I have found myself in several more since. Apparently, dating in your twenties can feel a little more like a situation every time, rather than something developing into a full-blown relationship.

One thing that separates a situationship from anything else is the pure lack of communication. This means you never truly know where you stand. You know you aren't friends, because you don't have sex with your friends, but you know you're not in a committed relationship. Again, like everything, there are pros and cons. So, let's delve a little deeper.

PROS OF A SITUATIONSHIP . . .

If you don't want anything serious, this is for you – When it comes to situations like these, there tends to be no seriousness involved. It can be a little confusing sometimes to know where you stand, but it's probably never going to grow into anything more, so sit back, relax, and enjoy the emotional rollercoaster.

If you're horny, this is *also* definitely for you – A lot of people know that situationships most probably involve a lot of sex. This is why friends with benefits sometimes turn into a situationship, because you'll just be seeing each other to have fun at first.

This leads me on to my cons list . . .

CONS OF A SITUATIONSHIP . . .

Someone always catches feelings – This is where the situation in situationship appears from. One person is always more likely to catch feelings, leading them to get hurt and left in a situation they never wanted to be in. If you feel like your situation is heading this way, the best thing you can do is be honest with the other person and say you're a little on the cautious side – this will prevent hate further down the line.

It most probably will be a waste of time – If that is what you want, then amazing, but often it's just wasting time that you could be spending on yourself, working on yourself, your hobbies, seeing friends and family, all to only end in hurt and heartbreak if you catch feelings and it doesn't work out. Situationships are most definitely not for the faint hearted, so enter them with caution.

Open relationships

Open relationships – a relationship in which both partners agree that each is allowed to explore sexual relations with other people.

Open relationships can be a very divisive topic, so Byron and I are going to both share our different, personal perspectives and what we have learnt speaking to others about their experiences with it.

Byron's POV

For me, an open relationship isn't something I've ever taken part in myself, but I feel like as a gay man it is something that isn't unfamiliar within the community. I have met a ton of people that are in open relationships that work well for them, I've also met others that have tried to open their relationship up to other sexual partners and it completely ruined what they had before. Part of me can see why it works for some people, as they may love the person they're with, but also time may have made their sex life seem dull, or they just don't meet each other's sexual needs (two bottoms don't make a top) or a spark may have been lost, yet their love for each other outside of the bedroom has not. I think you must allow yourself to look at sex as just sex. I understand that sex is a massive part of being in a relationship with another person and you may correlate a lot of your sex life to how much you love that person. However, I do think there is a difference in sex when it's with someone you love versus someone who is just experiencing the same release as you, for example, a one-night stand. I think I'm too much of a jealous person to see someone I love getting pleasure from someone else. Yet I do think if you're able to explore with your partner and allow each other to experience new things that neither of you may have experienced before it could be quite fun, and the open communication of trust through the experience could even bring you closer together. But on the flip side it could turn you into a jealous psychopath (me).

I heard someone recently talk about how they believe 'opening a relationship is holding onto someone that doesn't want you, just giving them the green light to do what they would single' or 'to avoid them cheating' – because if you have that agreement then how can someone cheat, right? That is not a reason I think a couple should explore an open relationship. I think that is the other person looking for an excuse or a reason to hold on to the other person for longer, as they are not quite ready to let them go. I think people that do have a successful open relationship understand their love for their partner and their sexual desires as two different things, or sometimes the same thing but with the ability to separate the two when necessary. Of course, this all needs to be talked about and maybe decide on a list of dos and don'ts so you can make sure everyone involved feels respected. I do think if this is all done correctly it is possible for it to work for some people, just maybe don't use opening your relationship as a last resort to keep someone in your life that doesn't want to be there anymore.

Anastasia's POV

Personally, open relationships would be something I would steer clear of. I have developed a few trust issues within my dating journey, and when I am dating someone I want to be with them and only them, and I want them to want me and only me. I don't disagree with them, and I think if couples can make it work and are happy with it working, then good for them! I just would not be suggesting this to my partner, and if they suggested it to me, I would see it as a problem, and would maybe feel like I wasn't good enough.

When I went on a cruise, I was very surprised to see that it's hugely common for people in open relationships to go on holidays like this in order to sleep with other couples. I got speaking to a man around the pool who was interested in one of my friends, and he continued to tell me that he had been married to his husband for over 15 years, but in the last three years they had opened their sexual relationship up to sleep with other men, or other gay couples. He said that after 12 years the sex got boring, and they are both completely okay with each other doing it. He then introduced me to his husband who told me a very similar story, and they had a great holiday. It was only when I was home that I found out about a particular type of party on the ship that couples in the bigger rooms were apparently throwing for other couples to go to so they could sleep with each other. Each night they would set the dress code as something different, so you would know who was interested in exploring further, and who wasn't. Saffron told me that one evening when her mum and dad were having drinks on the top deck, another couple came over to her mum, because she was wearing a dress covered in fruits. She then asked if her and Darren were interested, to which they turned around and asked what for. The couple apologised for their mistake and explained that the chosen dress code that night was items with fruit on, so Wendy had been mistaken for wanting to participate! Apparently there was a couples group chat where the dress code was advertised for all the participating couples to see. We had no idea this was going on, so it must have been very discreet, but apparently a lot of the people on board that night were wearing fruits. Unfortunately, Wendy did it on the wrong evening!

Friends with benefits

What a situationship often begins as: friends with benefits. I haven't really been in just a friend with benefits situation, as I have always ended up taking it a step too far and catching feelings, however, if I could be in a friend with benefits situation and not fall in love, it is something I would consider. Saffron has been a successful friend with benefits, so they can work.

In Saffron's situation, she was best friends with him before they decided to explore the sexual side of things, so I think this is why it worked. He started going over to hers a lot and they would sleep with each other, but then they started to go on dates, and cook dinner together, have sleepovers, but none of it was ever spoken about. It went on for a few months, but because they were friends before, doing things like cooking dinner together wasn't out of the ordinary, so it genuinely was friends with benefits. Before we went away for a month together, as he was dropping her to the airport, he decided to ask her what was going on. What a time to have a conversation like that, five minutes before you are about to catch an 11-hour flight! They both agreed they were on the same page, but this was the last time that they slept together, and they have remained good friends since.

I think their pre-existing friendship allowed for them to end on good terms and not catch feelings. When you meet someone in a club, you're meeting them for the first time, and you're naturally more likely to gain romantic feelings for them because most people jump the gun and ignore the fact you need to be friends first. Building that friendship with someone first is great, it's just important to know before you start sleeping with them if one of you is likely to gain feelings, because you don't want to lose the great friendship that you had to begin with, all for the sake of having sex a few times.

Another one of my best friends has been in a friend with benefits situation, but she caught feelings. We had met this group of boys in Albert's Schloss one night – and no, they weren't recruitment guys, as typically expected from this bar. They were lovely, and she really hit it off with one of them. A few months later, she was moving into a new apartment building, and on her move-in day, she saw him in the lobby. They found out they were living on the same floor, as next-door neighbours – it was basically the perfect set-up for her, a f*** buddy next door. Or so she first thought. She went round several times, and they had some wild sex. I guess this is what friends with benefits is all about, exploring your wildest sexual fantasies and testing the waters on what you like and don't like. She liked sleeping with him a lot, and started to grow fond of him, as more than a friend. He then started to turn a little weird and would flake on her very last-minute. As they lived next door, she could easily see who was going in and out of his flat, not in a stalker way, but come on – it's perfect if you want to spy on someone! Her flatmate had said to her that she had previously seen a girl go in and out of his flat a few times within the last few weeks, which technically should be fine as they had no ties, they were just friends with benefits – however, this obviously upset her. After being ignored and cancelled on several times, she decided to ask what was going on, and to her shock she was still ignored. Around three months later when we were away on a work trip, she got a phone call from another one of our friends. She had just found out that he had a girlfriend all along and he had in fact moved to London with her, out of the flat next door. This is an example of when friends with benefits goes wrong, because one of them caught feelings, and this is what you need to look out for if you find yourself in one of these situations, especially if you're with someone who is not honest from the beginning.

Keeping it in the friendship . . .

A bit of an inside joke within my friendship group is that I always like to, well, keep it inside the friendship group. This story I haven't shared with anyone before, despite people having their suspicions about it for the last few years on social media, because it's always felt a little too personal. But if I am going to tell it anywhere, it is here.

So, Byron and I. Yes, the same Byron who has been writing in this book, my best friend. We have had history, and there was a period in our lives where everything got a little complicated with us, which dare I say neither of us probably expected. Starting from the very beginning, I met Byron at a YouTuber event called Soccer Six when I was 15, so we have known each other over eight years. We had barely spoken but we had exchanged a few messages on Twitter beforehand. He forever claims that I messaged him on Twitter asking for him to come down and meet me at this event, however, until he provides receipts for this accusation, I don't recall. A few months later, I went to stay with Haz, who happened to live in the university dorm room next to him. He said that he didn't think he was going to get on with me very well because he couldn't judge my sense of humour off my videos, so we were both already going into this a little nervous. To his surprise, we hit it off straight away and I ended up staying in his bed that night instead of Haz's, and we top and tailed and watched an episode of *Love Island*. From here, our friendship really blossomed, and I felt like I had met someone I was going to know for the rest of my life. I can't explain the feeling, it was just different.

A few years passed, and Haz and Byron moved into a house in London, where I basically also lived – they even gave me my own shelf in the fridge – but I wasn't paying any rent. I truly had the best of both worlds with this one. I always ended up sleeping in Byron's bed, because we would stay up until a stupid hour messing around and Haz and Freya would want to sleep. One night, we had all been out, and I climbed into Byron's bed and rolled over to the opposite side to go to sleep. I felt him tickle my back, but I didn't respond. I think part of me thought, *Is he tickling my back, or am I imagining it?*, and the other part of me also didn't know how to react. We didn't speak about it the next morning, so I just carried on with my day and went with the option of pretending like it never happened. I told Haz he'd done this, then a few weeks later, he mentioned it to me and said he did tickle my back, so then I started to question what exactly was going on. Some time went by, nothing happened, and then he and Haz moved to Manchester. I so badly wanted to move but it was so far away from home, so I would go and stay a few times. I went up for his birthday, and we all went out that night and got a little too drunk. This is where it all started.

I say this is where it all started, but I still don't exactly know how this full night went down as we'd had a lot to drink. We were all having pre-drinks in his kitchen, and he put the phone down in front of us both to make a TikTok. He turned the sound down so I couldn't hear what it was until he uploaded it, but it was the song 'Birthday Sex'. When I saw it, I honestly thought it was one big joke, but apparently not. We went out that night, and Byron got VERY drunk and ended up going home early. I stayed out with our friends and one of his best friends, Ella, sat and spoke to me at the bar, and we talked about what would happen if I was to sleep with Byron. We didn't really come to any conclusion, so I guess I was just going to have to find out for myself. When I got back home later that evening, I climbed into his bed, then one thing led to another and we slept with each other. When I woke up the next morning, I walked out of his bedroom into the living room where everyone was patiently waiting to find out what had happened, and of course I was facing everyone alone because Byron had decided to have a lie-in. I was originally thinking about keeping it a secret, and not telling them we had slept together as I didn't in all honesty know what their reactions were going to be – however this was no longer an option, as Byron had bitten my lip so hard it looked like I had just got lip filler, so they all took one look at me and instantly knew. Everyone's reactions were nowhere near as bad as I had imagined in my head. Either way, their response would have been valid. It is stupidly complicated sleeping with a best friend; it could change not only the dynamic of the couple who are sleeping together, but also that of the whole friendship group, therefore it could be a selfish thing to do.

After telling everyone, Byron and I didn't speak about it in person. I think we both felt too awkward to address the elephant in the room, so when I left Manchester, he texted me and we spoke about it over message. We were all off on holiday to Santorini a few weeks after this, so I think we both were wondering who was staying in what bed when we went away. He sent me a message that read simply:

> 'Am I wrong in thinking we should pack condoms for Santorini?'

Well, that answered my question. The thing is, I was still so confused. Were we just sleeping together for the sake of being friends with benefits? Did he like me? Did I like him? I think at this point everything was so up in the air, I truly had no idea what was going on.

Fast-forward to Santorini, and we ended up staying in the same bed every night on this holiday. When we were chilling by the pool during the day, nothing would happen – no hints, no flirting – and none of our friends even mentioned it or made any jokes about it. But in the evening, things would switch up a little. One night we were lying in bed and everything got a little frisky, but we didn't end up having sex because we kept getting walked in on. So the following night, as we were alternating beds, we picked the bed in the living area, as if we wanted to do something, no one would hear. We decided to take it a step further, and instead of having sex in the house where we were at risk of getting found out, we went outside and had sex on the day beds overlooking the ocean. It probably is, to this date, one of the prettiest places I have ever had sex, and I think the thrill of knowing we shouldn't be doing this made it a little more exciting. We didn't sleep together again on that trip, and I kind of thought that would be the end of it.

A little deep, but a key part of the story is that before sleeping with Byron, I had only slept with one person, and was very scared of sleeping with someone again. I didn't have the best outlook on sex, as my first time was very different to what I had expected, so it had been a few years since I had been intimate with someone. That is probably the reason why I was able to open myself up in this way again with someone, because it was my best friend, so I didn't feel judged. I felt comfortable, and knew he was going to treat me with the respect I deserved.

He brought back my confidence in the bedroom, which is something I had really lacked for a few years, so even if nothing was going to come out of the situation on a romantic level, he had helped me in other ways more than he probably realised.

From Santorini, myself and two of my best friends, Haz and Freya, flew straight to Kavos for a little girls' trip off the back of the big group holiday. We were only going for four days but I was excited to be going away with just the girls, especially because I was confused as to what was going on between Byron and me, so this was the perfect time to sit down and talk to them about it. In a nutshell, they said we needed to stop before it went any further, and half of me agreed with them because I didn't want it to ruin the friendship, but the other half of me was enjoying myself for the first time in a long time, so didn't want it to end. When I went to Kavos, as Byron and I never spoke or discussed what was going on, in my head, I was single, had my confidence back, and was ready to enjoy having sex again. Haz and I ended up getting along well with two of the workers from one of the trips we did whilst out there, and as I was young and on a girls' holiday having fun, I decided to sleep with one of them. This was HUGE for me. I was absolutely terrified a few weeks before this to sleep with anyone again, and thanks to Byron, I finally felt like I could enjoy such a natural thing again. Now the not-fun part was telling Byron I had decided to sleep with someone else whilst away, so I texted him and told him just to get it out of the way, and in all honesty, he took it well. We weren't a 'thing', we were simply just friends sleeping with each other, so really, that was the only way I'd hoped he would take it.

When I arrived home, I stayed at Byron's for the night before travelling back to my house as we landed late at night, and I ended up sleeping with him, for the last time. We both lay in bed and agreed that this was the last time, and it wasn't going to happen again, simply because it couldn't. How had I gone from not having had sex for two to three years, to sleeping with two different people in the same week, oops!

A few weeks went on, and in all honesty, I was struggling with what Byron and I had done. I questioned myself, a lot. Do I like him? Do I regret sleeping with him because now I might be be jealous of his future partners? So many questions were spiralling in my head, and I was too afraid to ask him because I didn't want to make it awkward, or if it was one-sided, I might be embarrassed. Luckily, it wasn't, and he made the first move in speaking about it, thank God. He texted me a long paragraph, saying that he'd liked me like that for a long time, so I felt like I could admit that I had also really liked him for a long time. Being honest with each other felt good.

Now several years have passed, Byron and I have remained best friends, and we 100 per cent will for the rest of our lives. I guess in some ways it did affect our friendship, because whether we both want to admit it or not, I know that we will always feel something that tiny bit more for each other, despite being with other people and falling in love with others. I have a lot to thank Byron for; he made me realise a lot about myself, and I think I can safely say I did the same for him. Part of me used to think Byron will be the person that I would marry and have children with. We used to take pictures on every holiday we went on of him holding my belly as though I was pregnant. They say when you know, you just know, but now we've settled for being in each other's lives as just friends, we can carry on experiencing life together, making more memories and being proud of who each other is becoming, and who each other is choosing to love.

We have kissed a few times since sleeping together, though. Sorry for being so irresistible, Byron.

How do I know if I have found my soul mate?

First, do we think soul mates even exist? I would like to think that somewhere out there, one person within the 8 billion people living on this planet is my perfect match, but also I think there can be such things as friendship soul mates, not just romantic ones.

I have experienced somewhat of a soul mate connection in the past, or what I believe one to be. It's a feeling you get where you just know, you can't explain how, or why, you just do. It wasn't just that we connected in a sexual way, or that we had a few things in common which led to some great conversations, we connected on a level where I felt my soul bond with theirs. It's almost as though there is an invisible magnet pulling you towards each other and no matter how hard you try to pull away, a little part of you never can. To that person, you appear almost transparent, because they can see you better than you can sometimes see yourself and know how you're going to react to a situation before you even do yourself. You can sit in silence with that person for days on end, and you feel so content just being in their presence. You feel like you need to be with them all the time, because when you're together your souls are happy. It's an indescribable feeling of pure contentment, happiness and love, one that every single person deserves to experience.

There is also such a thing as a soul tie. This is a connection established between two people, in which the intense bond transcends your physical body and goes deep into the soul. These connections often form once you have had sex with someone, and can build far beyond the physical connection, deep into an emotional one too. This type of connection is something I also feel like I may have experienced, with the same person I consider my soul mate. But saying this, I do believe you can have several soulmates, I don't think it can just be one person. Some people meet their soul mate within the first few years of being born and grow up together; others won't cross paths with theirs until they are 70 and will forever wish they'd met earlier on in life; some people may never meet their soul mate and others could have multiple. But I believe that once you've met this person, or multiple people, it will take every bone in your body to stay away from them, and even if you split up, fall out, end up hating each other, ten years down the line you will still think of this person and wonder what they are doing, if they are safe, if they are happy.

Because once your soul connects with them, a little part of your soul switches with theirs and stays within you.

But friendship soul mates, these most definitely exist. I believe Byron is one of my friendship soul mates, because from the day we met each other it felt like we had met before. I find it hard to get comfortable with people quickly and am very wary of letting people get close to me in the fear of them hurting me or leaving, but when you meet a friendship soul mate, it's almost a gut-instinct feeling of knowing that's not the case, and you're safe to be completely and utterly you. Every time I experience anything fun, and every time I'm sad, he is the one person I want to pick up my phone and message to let him know, and the one person I want to help me. He's even sat next to me whilst I write this, because we can't really keep away from each other. It's a true blessing to have met him when I did, and growing up by his side is more than I could have ever wished for.

If you don't think you have met your soul mate yet, and don't really believe in them because of this, don't lose hope. I'm not entirely sure if I have met my soul mate on a romantic level yet, nor am I in a rush to. I believe you'll meet them when you least expect it and when the time is right for them to walk into your life – and when they do, don't fight the feeling. It's sometimes scary, and not what you think you want, but it's more than likely what you need.

Signs you're in a healthy relationship

I would say I had a healthy relationship with my ex-boyfriend, so a few thoughts here are from experience, but I have also witnessed the most beautiful relationship blossom between my best friend Haz and her new boyfriend. She has quite literally gone through it *all* with previous partners, a lot of which left her emotionally scarred and feeling like she would never be able to find a 'healthy' relationship, until she met her boyfriend on the flight as I explained a few chapters ago. This is the perfect example of if someone is meant to be in your life, and your paths are meant to cross, they will. The funny thing is, now they have been together over a year, they realised growing up they went to a lot of the same places, so it's more than likely they have seen each other before or been in the same place at the same time. The plane was just another one of the places their paths were destined to cross, because their souls needed to meet when they did. Anyway, since they began speaking, her boyfriend has truly shown her what it is like to be loved in a healthy, happy way, and in the way she has always deserved. So, this one is for you, Haz – watching you grow into the happiest version of yourself and seeing the smile come back onto your face has been everything. Thanks to you, this is how I know the signs you're in a healthy relationship . . .

Respect – Of course, for a relationship to work, you must have love, that is a given, but you must also have trust and respect. It's so important to respect each other's boundaries, each other's wishes, hopes and dreams for life and each other's beliefs, rights and traditions. Understanding these things about your partner is a key aspect to a healthy relationship and should be standard if you are wanting to spend the rest of your life with this person.

Communication – Communicating with your partner, and being honest, is also another big one. If you don't want to do something, tell them, and if you don't feel comfortable with something your partner is doing or saying, tell them. Nothing will get resolved if you don't speak openly to each other, and if the other person respects you enough, they will make every effort to change and make things better. Nothing can go wrong with communicating, as at least you have been honest and can hold your own within the relationship.

Supportive – There is nothing better than being supportive in a relationship and being your partner's number one fan. In everything they do, you should want to see them succeed and do anything you can to help this person reach their goals and desires. Even little things like being supportive of your partner's Saturday-night takeaway choice – let them have it occasionally!

Teamwork – I am a firm believer that once you are in a relationship with someone, you are a team, so when one person has a problem, it becomes a problem for both of you to resolve. You become a team if you decide to start a family together, or if you support each other's decisions. Whatever you decide to become a team in, this is a big sign you're in a healthy relationship, knowing that no matter what, your teammate will always be there.

You still have *your* life – One of the biggest signs you're in a healthy relationship is that you still have your own separate life, whilst being with your partner. As couples are together for longer, move in with each other and start a family, naturally your lives merge together, but it's SO important to still go out and do things with your friends without your partner being there, or taking yourself out on a solo date to go and get a coffee. Whatever it is, keeping that little part of you separate will help the relationship grow more positively in a healthy direction.

All the above are just a few pointers that I think are key for a relationship to go the distance. These things don't have to necessarily be present right from the start, and some may go wrong and need fixing or working on, and that is okay. No relationship is ever perfect, and there are always going to be little problems that crop up at times even in the most perfect relationship. What I have learnt is that relationships take time and effort to build, and even if at times it feels hard, and almost like it's not worth it, it is often just on the other side of this feeling where the relationship truly blossoms.

Diary Entry

Ending this chapter on a slightly high note, I received something I just had to write about, because it really is giving old-school romance and something I *never* thought a boy would do for me. I got a love letter. What the f***? I have always been one to fall for romance in this way — cute little letters around the house, flowers, them opening the door for me, little things which to them might not mean a lot, but for me go a long way. Well, the only slight plot twist is the love letter is in fact from my ex-boyfriend. We aren't together, so it did come as a bit of a shock when I opened and read the words, but despite the timing, the words were truly beautiful and the fact he remembered what I wore when we first met (he wrote this in the letter) really made me smile. Like I said, it's the little things. I'm still very single, with no new boys in my DMs, or on my Hinge, which is a bit of a shock, but it feels weirdly good right now, and almost right, to be single. I can't imagine myself in a relationship at this stage of my life, but who knows, maybe I'll bump into my soul mate when I get off this flight to LA?

As you're reading this book, I hope it is becoming more evident that the happier you are within yourself, and the more content you are with your own life, the happier your relationship with other people will be, and your relationship is more likely to go the distance. I don't want you to feel disheartened if you don't think you have encountered your soul mate yet, or if your relationship isn't going how you had hoped it would. No matter how old you are, where you are at in your life, or who you are currently with, everything happens for a reason, and is happening exactly how it should. Often, when things occur in life, the reason is never apparent at that moment but becomes clear as time goes on.

Chapter 7

The Breakup

ONE OF THE reasons you might be reading this book is because you have gone through a breakup, or are going through one as we speak, and you are looking for that light at the end of the tunnel that everyone claims there is. Even if it doesn't feel like it in the moment, or for a long time after, that old saying is true: time is just the biggest healer and you must trust that over time you'll find that light. Breakups aren't easy, but sometimes they must happen even if you don't want them to, to benefit yourself and allow you to grow because the relationship is no longer serving you. So let's delve into the gruesome details and find a way, together, to navigate a breakup.

Knowing when to let go

Sometimes the reason you need to let go is clear. Your partner may have been disloyal and cheated, you might have become two completely different people compared to when you first met and are no longer a match, or sometimes it just isn't working but you aren't entirely sure why.

I have had a very hard time knowing when to let go of situations that no longer meet my expectations. I often give people the benefit of the doubt or try to put myself in their shoes to understand why they are acting in a certain way, but after a while neither of these things makes it any better, and it reaches the point where letting go is truly the only option. I have had two situations and relationships I have needed to let go of to become a better person and move forward. Sometimes this doesn't mean you have to let go of the person completely and never have them in your life again, it just means you need to let go of the situation you have both found yourselves in, and if that means going no contact, not speaking for years, or somehow remaining friends throughout – you'll know the best way for you to handle it.

I never felt like I got closure from my situationship, which made it that little bit harder for me to let go; however, with my last relationship I knew everything I needed to know, so moving forward seemed a little easier. I am just the sort of person that needs the *information* for me to be able to compute it inside my brain, otherwise I will go off on a million and one tangents in my head and make up the most insane scenario, truly believing that is what happened. Oh, I love being a girl.

It's funny, having to let go of two romantic situations in my life in the last few years has given me a bit of a complex. Before being in a situation, I would have died to have been in love. The thought of loving someone unconditionally and having a partner for life filled me with warmth and joy. Now I have been hurt, the thought of being in love again kind of makes me want to die. It's an emotional juxtaposition, one that I am working on resolving, but one that is taking a lot more work than I first thought.

But you're probably still wondering, how do *you* know when to let go? I think you just know. There comes a time in your relationship, or situation, where something can't be worked on, and the relationship is no longer serving your life the way it positively should, and it becomes a fight. You want it to work but sometimes the side of putting yourself first is what you should be fighting for.

You feel unfulfilled – When you are with your partner, you should feel as though they are adding happiness and contentment to your life, and the minute this is disrupted things start to change. Being in a relationship should fulfil you, and once you feel like it is no longer doing that, it is a sign that you should think about moving on. Life is too short to stay in something that isn't choosing you and helping you become a better version of yourself, so take this as a major flag to assess where you are at and consider if you would be happier without them.

Your needs are no longer being met – This was one of the reasons I broke something off with someone, because I didn't feel like what I needed in that situation was a priority for the other person anymore. For something to work, you must meet each other's needs, and if they are no longer meeting yours, even after trying, it's time to start letting go.

They are ruining your peace – When trying to keep someone in your life is ruining your peace, it's time to stop. Your peace is always more important than their presence, and when you do find someone they will add to your peace, not destroy it. It's not easy to let go when it reaches this point, and in some ways this is the worst way to lose someone, because you know you need to let them go, but don't want to.

Handling the breakup

Now we've covered some reasons why you should let go; we need to cover the actual breakup. Not the cutest part, I must admit. I think some people are good at handling breakups, and others not so much – I slot into the 'not so much' category.

When you have broken up with someone, there are five stages of the breakup that you are possibly going to go through, which are also the five stages of grief. When you are no longer in a relationship, you are essentially going to be grieving someone who is still alive and grieving the situation you were once in, so it will probably start with ...

Denial – The stage where you will tell yourself you have made the wrong decision or deny having broken up at all. It is the way your brain deals with unwanted news. You aren't ready to accept the situation, so it is much easier to deny its existence.

Anger – When denial starts to fade, anger comes into its place. You might not even feel angry directly at your ex, more so the situation, but this is a common emotion after the breakup. In this stage, you want to ensure you are not making any hasty decisions or doing things you may regret – instead try to put your energy into something beneficial for you.

Bargaining – The middle stage, where you're going to start feeling like you should reconnect with that person now the anger has gone, even if it is just as a friendship.

Depression – Whether you decide to rebuild a friendship or have decided against that, reality is going to hit, and you are simply going to feel sad. It almost feels like at this point you are grieving your relationship and grieving someone that is still alive, but turning this sadness into reflection is the best way forward. Reflect on what you can do to become a better person and how you can carry everything you have learnt in your previous relationship into your next.

Acceptance – The final stage of the breakup, where you will be okay with what has happened and ready to move on from the situation. It is normal to want to keep a loved one in your heart forever, especially if you spent a long time with them, but accepting that it is in the past and not meant for your future is the healthiest way to accept the breakup and grow as an individual.

Now we've covered the stages, let's delve a little deeper into what you can do to help yourself through them . . .

You must go NO CONTACT – If you are wanting to handle this breakup in the healthiest way possible, deciding to go no contact, even if it is just for a set amount of time, is one of the best ways to deal with it. I don't think you can truly move on from someone you cared about or loved whilst still speaking to them every day, because it will be a constant reminder of that person and in some ways might feel like you haven't even broken up. No contact is hard – you may feel lost or lonely, like it is the wrong decision, but as time goes on, as long as you don't give into your impulsive decisions, or go on a night out, get drunk and decide to booty call them, you will thank yourself for this one.

Understand it's okay to not be okay – A lot of the time after breakups, people rush into thinking they will magically be okay in a matter of days, which for the majority is not the case. On the other hand, some people think they will never be okay again, which is also not the case. Healing doesn't have a time scale; you can't pick a date and say you're going to be okay by then, because you might not be. The best way to deal with a breakup in this sense is understand that time heals everything, but time doesn't have a scale or use-by date. Don't be angry at yourself for feeling and allowing yourself to feel, because being able to feel so deeply for someone or a situation is truly a blessing. Feel everything.

Change your surroundings – No, I don't mean fully up and leave your current living situation and move into a whole new house, but it wouldn't hurt to change some things around. Feeling like you are in a fresh new space, even if it is just changing your bed sheets, will help prevent your mind from constantly reminding you of the past.

Don't be afraid to talk about your feelings – There is nothing worse than bottling up everything you are feeling inside of you until you hit breaking point and it bursts. Talking to people, family, friends, a therapist, or even making a voice note to yourself to say the feelings and words out loud, will help you come to terms with them. You should never feel stupid for wanting to talk about how you feel, nor should you feel like no one around you cares, because everyone does, and everyone is rooting for you to come out of the breakup happy.

There are, of course, other things you can do to handle the breakup in a healthy way, such as keeping yourself busy, looking for new activities to do, getting yourself out for walks, cooking yourself good meals etc., but the reality of a breakup for some people isn't that and it is a lot easier said than done. Don't put too much pressure on yourself to do all this too quickly; do it when *you* feel ready, everyone is different.

Relationship breakup vs situationship breakup

Why does it feel like breaking up from a situationship is technically harder than breaking up from your actual relationship? I weirdly have experienced this, and for many months I have tried to figure out why this is, and I think I finally have.

It all comes down to your attachment style. Attachment styles are something I have had to do a little research on whilst dating as I at first didn't realise it was a thing, but it explains a lot about why people can behave differently when they're in relationships.

Secure – This style is very warm, trusting and forgiving. You have good boundaries set with each other and can both manage your emotions well, which results in you always being open and honest with each other.

Anxious – You have a lot of relationship-related insecurities and you fear abandonment, you lack boundaries and are sensitive to every emotion. You might find yourself over-accommodating the other person's needs to make them happy, putting their happiness above your own.

Avoidant – You fear being close to this person, and often act distant. In these relationships you don't want conflict and will avoid it at all costs, whilst also being emotionally distant. You could call it independence, but on an extreme scale.

Disorganised – Often, this sort of style means you find intimacy and trust difficult with your person, and you'll find yourself dissociating from situations. You want to be close to them, but you are fearful of others and lack empathy in the situation.

When you are in a situationship, due to the lack of understanding as to where you stand, it is more common to develop an unhealthy attachment style, often an anxious one, and when the situation ends it is extremely painful because it confirms a fear deep within a person that has never hit the surface before – that someone they care about will one day abandon them, and unexpectedly leave. In a situationship, the fun part, or not-so-fun a lot of time, is the unknown – you never know if it is going to turn into something more or if it's just temporary, therefore these feelings naturally consume your body more and more. In the course of one day you can go from speaking about marriage and children to being blocked and ghosted, yet the other person technically doesn't owe you an explanation because you were not officially together. Because of this, there is a natural feeling of wanting to know why didn't it work out. Why didn't they want me? Have they found someone they think is better than me? These sorts of unanswered questions and feelings can subconsciously scar a person and leave a mark on them forever going into future relationships.

By contrast, most of the time when you are in a relationship you will probably have felt when it might be coming to an end. In a relationship you have already committed to each other, you know that love is or was mutually there for each other so there is no guessing game to be had. You might have also had several discussions before about it not working out, so when it does come to an end, it isn't completely unexpected, and a lot of the time you will begin to move on from that person whilst still being with them, so it doesn't hurt as much when it truly does end.

This is what happened to me. When I was in a situationship, I had no idea what was going to come of it or if anything was going to come of it all because he never expressed how he felt to me, hence why I decided to end things. Whereas when I was with my ex-boyfriend, I knew he loved me and I never had to question that, therefore my attachment style was different. When I was in a relationship, I had a mix of secure but also avoidant at the same time. The avoidant style developed from my situation before, where I had an anxious attachment. An anxious style is common when you don't know where you stand, and unfortunately did lead me to developing further issues in my subsequent relationship. Becoming aware of this has completely changed my outlook on how I would go forward dating now, though, and I am aware that I need to work on a few scars that have been left, but becoming aware is the first step to being okay.

Closure

Do you really need closure to move on from a situation? Closure is what a lot of people crave to shut off from a relationship, situation or chapter of their life. It is associated with being the end of something, so without closure it's sometimes hard to accept that it is truly the end.

From experience, I do understand the need for closure. I went a year with no contact with someone, and even though as time went on I began to care less, and it was no longer at the forefront of my mind, occasionally it would crop up again and I would wonder what had gone on and was that really the end. When I eventually spoke to this person again, I was worried that everything I felt prior would resurface and essentially take me back to stage one, however, because of how long it had been and how much self-improvement I had undergone in the lead-up, it didn't affect me in the way I thought it would. This was a positive thing for me to see, and it showed me that I have emotionally matured and moved on from the situation romantically, and confirmed that I no longer wanted to be with this person.

I know that for a lot of people, closure can also be a painful thing. Sometimes the closure you hoped for isn't what you have been served with, and if you'd hoped you'd get back with someone and instead find out they have moved on with a new partner and have no interest in rekindling the relationship, it will probably hurt. However, at the same time this would force you into the mindset – well, eventually – that this relationship no longer serves you, and there is better on the other side.

A few of my friends have gone through some intense relationships and situations followed by horrendous breakups, so I thought it would be interesting to hear their thoughts on closure.

FREYA'S PAST DATES

First we have Freya. Freya is one of my best friends and hasn't made romance or boys the focal point of her twenties, which I think is quite a rarity nowadays. She is 25 and has only slept with one person (who she went on two dates with) and has only ever gone on dates with two people. I like this example because even though Freya hasn't been in a relationship, or necessarily been heartbroken, she still felt like she needed closure from the first person she went on a few dates with and slept with, as it was her first experience entering the dating world, and one she will always remember. With the person she slept with, things ended quickly as Freya was moving to Manchester and he was based over three hours away, so she didn't want anything serious. But from sleeping with him and trying dating, she said she realised she wasn't ready for it, and needed to focus on herself and bettering how she felt so that she could eventually be ready to let someone in again and share those moments with another person. When I asked her how she got closure, she doesn't necessarily think she did. Her closure was found from within, and now she is in a much better place in terms of how she views herself. However, a common theme is, they *always* come back. Freya heard from this boy again a few years after and decided not to reply. For her this was a lesson, a chapter, and that chapter is now closed. He was a part of her finding herself and that is all the closure she needed.

HAZ'S PAST RELATIONSHIP

Haz being okay with talking to me about this particular experience and allowing me to write about it is a big step forward in her gaining closure, and for that, I will be endlessly proud of her. She was sadly in an abusive relationship, unknown to all of us, for ten months of her twenties, and gaining closure from this is quite something to have to do for anyone, especially someone so young. When I asked her if she had gained closure from the situation, she said she never really got any until she found her beautiful new relationship. Now she knows what true love is and how a relationship should be, she can see that what she had before was far from true love, and this has given her closure to know that she is now in the right place and that it ended at the right time for her to be where she is today. She's always wanted to be a singer, so she writes music about her experience in that previous relationship, which also could be seen as a form of closure. Processing the situation in this way has given her her own type of closure, without the need to get it from him.

If you think you might be in an abusive relationship, it is so important to reach out to someone that you trust, such as a close friend or a charity like Women's Aid, who provide support services and guidance. They can also provide information on how to support a friend who has confided in you about being in an abusive relationship. It takes a lot of courage and strength to speak out, and the more we can do to support one another, the better.

MY MUM'S PAST RELATIONSHIP

Even though this book is focused on modern-day dating, having a point of view from someone who has experienced dating for the last 30 years, and has gone through several rounds of letting go and closure might give our generation an idea of how to deal with it, or in my mum's case, how to live with it. For background context, she was with my biological father for a few months when she fell pregnant with me, and then he left her, so she became a single mum. She then met my stepfather, who was our next-door neighbour. We lived with my nan at the time and my mum asked him to put together some of my toys for my first Christmas and the rest is history. They got married and were together for around nine years, and then split. She then had a situationship with a man who it turned out had a wife the entire time, after which she fell pregnant with Atticus with her boyfriend of a few months, who then left. She has never truly had luck in love but she reminds me every day that even though she is growing older, she still has hope that her soul mate is out there. As you can imagine, the closure my mum once craved and thought she needed would have been extreme, from one situation to the next, but when I asked her, she said to me:

> I have made peace with myself over the last few years, which has given me closure without directly receiving it from everyone who has done me wrong or every situation I was in. When I was your age, I was very up and down and emotional – everything always seemed such a drama – but as I have got older, I have realised that the feelings don't change, but your approach to them does. I now put myself first. Don't get me wrong, you still feel the occasional sting from time to time, but having you and Atticus has healed that, and I make peace with the situations for my children.

I had a feeling she was going to say something like this, because I have realised as I have been getting older, you do just learn to make peace with situations. Life has dealt my mum some awful cards in the relationship sector, but it makes me so happy to know my little brother and I have helped her heal and she now sees peace in the situation.

GIVING CLOSURE TO SOMEONE ELSE

Wanting closure from someone is one thing but being emotionally strong enough to give someone else closure is a whole other level. This is something that I am still figuring out how to do, because to give closure to someone else I fear you need a certain level of it within yourself and the situation – therefore it can be deemed a vicious cycle.

One thing you can do to give someone the closure they need is to simply *talk to them*. Answering any questions that they have truthfully and giving them time to vent to you can help them move on and receive closure from your end: it truly is all based on honesty if that is what they need.

The main point in giving closure to someone is always being willing to give it. A lot of the time people don't want to do this because subconsciously they are not ready for the chapter to end, but this is all part of learning about and navigating the dating world.

Getting under to get over . . .

Let's switch up the mood and talk about a little something we like to call the *rebound*. Everyone has probably had one at some stage, and they can come in all different forms, some not always that obvious.

Type #1 – This sort of rebound can just be someone you are texting to fill the gap. You miss telling someone about your day or giving you the odd compliment, so texting someone can make you feel like nothing has changed.

Type #2 – A dating app match. I can't lie, I have done this one – matching with someone on a dating app for a cheeky bit of validation then arranging to meet them just for attention. Admitting that is not cute but keeps you in the dating world and takes your mind off what's really going on.

Type #3 – An ex. It's not uncommon to reach out to a previous ex when you are going through a breakup. Losing someone can sometimes make you miss other people from your past, so when they say exes come back, it's probably because they have just lost what they left you for and are living in regret.

Type #4 – A one-night stand with a random person you've never met, and never plan on seeing again. Probably the best kind if you do not want things to get messy. Is this actually a good idea? At the time, probably. A few months down the line, probably not. I have only ever had one rebound situation in my time, but I never actually slept with them, I just went on a date, the day after a talking stage with another boy ended. I was in my feels and was most definitely looking for attention as I was still in disbelief over what had happened. Whilst I was in that talking stage with the other guy, a boy – a beautiful boy may I add – had messaged me asking if I wanted to go on a date but as I was talking to someone else, I never replied. Well, now I was freshly single, the day after I thought I would respond, and it turns out he was in Manchester for work, so he asked me to go get food with him. I went and, as nice as it was to meet him in person, it only made me feel worse once I had left because it wasn't who I wanted to be going on a date with at the time. So maybe a rebound within 24 hours is not quite the route I would recommend going down.

However, for others, a rebound is exactly what some

people need. I'm talking about the healthiest version of a rebound there is, which I would say is going out and ending up with someone you have no history with, because rebounding with an ex is only going to cause you double the heartbreak. I know someone who ended up having a rebound with their neighbour, and it was *exactly* what they needed. They had just left a year-long relationship and so had their neighbour, who, can I add, was giving PURE sex appeal. One glass of wine led to the full bottle, and then the rest is history. In this case, getting under someone helped her get over someone else, but I think she got lucky, he probably just knew what he was doing – unlike her sh**y ex. The other reason this probably worked was because they both knew the situation they were getting themselves into, rather than planning a full-blown date which would result in a dead end.

Serious talk: sleeping with someone to try to get over someone else can be messy, and it can also end in tears. It might make you realise how much you miss the other person and just how *not* ready you are to move on with someone else. For me, having sex is a very personal thing, and even though when I was younger I did have some fun, as I have got older I have realised this sort of fun doesn't interest me as much anymore. As of when I am writing this, I have only built up an intimate sexual relationship with two people in the past, and I want to do that again with someone else going forward. After waiting months to even sleep with my ex-boyfriend, I want to wait until I meet someone who is going to treat me and my sexual needs as something special, instead of me just sleeping with someone to cover the hurt from my past.

On the other hand, if you want to go and sleep with other people to get over your ex or just because *you* want too, you go, just do it safely, and with care. Sex is something to be enjoyed for both men AND women, there is no shame in enjoying a natural part of life.

Moving forward and setting boundaries

After a breakup, a lot of things tend to become clear as to what you would no longer accept in a relationship, and what you now want in your next relationship. A few things I think are important for a relationship in your twenties are . . .

Balance – As most people experience their first relationship during these years, it is so easy to get swept away in the excitement of it all and forget that these are also some of the best years of your life to go out with your friends and have fun, as well as figuring out what you want to do with your career. Ensure that as well as working on your relationship you are remembering to work on yourself and your future goals.

Loyalty – This might sound like a given at this point, but it's true. After going through many failed talking stages and always finding out I am, essentially, the other woman, I'm setting a few personal red lines in my next relationships. I truly believe that if they like you enough, they will be loyal to you and only you from pretty much the beginning.

Drive – One of the most important things in my life is my career and ensuring all my dreams come true. When moving forward with a new partner, I want my career to still be my number one focus and drive in life, and my partner to support this decision. They should push you to be your best every single day, just as much as you push yourself. Drive doesn't have to be career-based, however; drive can extend way past this and be seen in every single aspect of your life, hence why I think it's an important quality to have.

The exes

We've spoken about closure, moving forward and setting new boundaries, but are you really over your ex? Or does a little part of you still believe that one day you are going to rekindle, and everything is going to go back to how it was?

Re-dating an ex is always a tricky path to go down because, yes, on the one hand it could work perfectly, as the time you both spent separate from each other could have made you grow as individuals so that you can now come back to each other and grow as one. However, it could also go the opposite way as nothing may have changed, so getting back with them or giving things another go could be taking a step backwards and only lead to prolonged heartache down the line.

Have I ever re-dated an ex? *No.*

Do I plan on re-dating one my exes? *Not anymore.*

I say not anymore because I have pondered this for many months, but I am a strong believer that they are an EX for a reason. It's a little bit different with my last ex-boyfriend, because he genuinely did nothing wrong at all. He only ever showed me unconditional love and wanted to put me first above everything, but sadly I was just not at a place in my life where I felt ready for that sort of love and commitment. I toyed with the idea of getting back together with him for months. For someone to be so persistent with me, I was adamant that they had been heaven-sent to show me what it is like to really be loved, cared for and respected. In some ways I feel like I manifested that because I would consistently say out loud, 'I won't accept anything less going forward,' and look at what I was served with. But despite this, it seems I was not ready to welcome that with open arms at that time. So, yes, for a while I did think about giving things another go and getting back with him, because it was giving 'right person, wrong time'. But I also believe that everything happens for a reason, and him being sent was to show me that what I wanted I will be able to get, when I am ready for it ... Or plot twist, I do get back with him and ignore my own advice. Who knows at this point?

Let's look at the pros and cons of re-dating one of your exes ...

PROS

You're already comfortable with each other – You know each other very well by this point, so I doubt there will be any awkward silences or uncertainty in what to say next. As you are starting again you might also feel those butterflies once more, especially if you never wanted to break up in the first place, in which case the excitement will be unmatched.

You've seen each other at your worst – You've probably had your first argument, you probably know when your partner wants to be left alone for some quiet time, and you probably know what things they love and hate by now, so you know what to expect when getting back with this person. You're not walking into this situation blindly, and getting the worst out of the way might even mean you get to enter the honeymoon phase again; everyone loves it in there.

You clearly can't keep away from each other – If both of you are wanting to give things another shot, there is obviously something very special between you both. Even if it doesn't work out the second time around, the fact that you were both willing to give it another shot and loved each other enough to not want to let each other go, should be seen as a good thing. I believe in second chances, but never thirds.

CONS

You might return to old habits – There must have been a reason for you to break up in the first place – something went wrong, you were on two different pathways, someone cheated. You don't want to end up in a vicious cycle of things continuously returning to the way they were, because if this is the case, there is no point giving the relationship a round two.

Forgiving is easier than forgetting – Whatever the reason was for the breakup, unless it was right person wrong time I'm sure it is something that you needed to forgive them for, and forgiving is easier than forgetting. Sometimes you think you have forgotten something, but getting back with that person will be a constant reminder of whatever happened and may bring all those feelings to the surface again. If you are going to give it another go, it is not healthy to live in the past, so ensure you are fully healed and moved on from it before you step into the future.

You may now lack security – As you have now gone through a breakup with each other, naturally even though you still feel the love and a sense of comfort with one another, you may no longer feel the security. Feeling secure and trusting your partner in a relationship are two key elements for it working out, so when you lack these, love is no longer enough.

If getting back with your ex isn't on the cards for whatever reason, another good way to let out pent-up emotions and feelings that you never got to share is by writing a letter to your ex, but not posting it to them. This is kind of like a diary entry, just one addressed to someone else instead, and when I have done this in the past, the emotional release you feel once you have signed the bottom of that letter is almost like letting go of that chapter of your life and signing it so you can't go back on it. The beauty of this is that no one else is ever going to read it, so you can go as hard, horrible or honest as you wish.

I didn't think anyone else would read my letter to my ex, but writing this book has given me the confidence to share parts of it with you, as mine ended up being more of a thank you, rather than an 'I hate you'.

> Part of me hates the fact that we met when we did, because it felt like a kick in the teeth from life saying: 'Here is what you have always wanted, but you can't quite have it yet, you're not ready.' That hurt. I tried to force myself to be ready because I was so desperate to feel what it was like to be in a relationship and be loved the way I deserved, and it felt exactly how I wanted it to feel, but instead you were living proof that someone can show you all the love and care in the world, but unless you love yourself enough, you can't accept that love from anyone else.
>
> I felt scarred from my previous experiences with boys. It was weird to me to be someone's main priority, and part of me feels guilty that I was unable to give you the love in return that you deserved. But I also wish I could thank you one more time for the love you did show me, for the patience, for the respect. You truly restored my faith in dating and, well, men, and when I am ready to get out there again, whenever that

may be, I will no longer feel as scared as I once did and that is all because of you.

If you can stay friends with an ex, were you truly in love with them?

I'm not sure. I have conflicting opinions on this because I've been in both situations, completely cutting contact during the grieving period in order to remain friends at a later date, and also remaining friends with someone while we both healed. From my situation where I had to cut contact, I knew I had to do that because he moved straight on with a new girl, so seeing or hearing about that when I was still hurting would have only ended up hurting me more. But reflecting on the situation, I know now that I loved the idea of him but I wasn't in love with him – and there is a big difference. I went into it with the fear that he never could love me, so I never let myself love him.

On the other hand, I have stayed friends with my ex-boyfriend since we broke up, and the longest we've gone without speaking is just under a week. Maybe this was because I was never deeply in love with him, again because I never let myself be. But I also think it is easier to be friends with someone when you are the one who is splitting up with the other person, because you are mentally prepared to let that person go if you are making the decision to break up with them anyway.

Before deciding if you should stay friends with an ex, let's have a look at some of the reasons why this might not benefit you.

Someone *still* has feelings – It would be a very perfect but rare situation for both of you to be able to switch from relationship to friendship and drop all the romantic stuff, but, from experience, if you are staying friends with an ex, one of you is most definitely in their feels still, and being friends is not going to help that. If you are the one who no longer has feelings, but your ex is persisting on being friends, the kindest thing to do is give it some time before rekindling a friendship. It is just impossible to heal with the constant reminder of that person.

You probably still want to sleep with them – Sleeping with your ex all the time is not cute or fun unless you have genuine intentions of getting back with them. You can't really just be friends if you are booty calling him at 3am after a Saturday night when you're drunk and bored. This is common even if you aren't friends, so be careful crossing this line again as it's not going to help the healing process.

You're still going to feel protective over them – Even if this person has hurt you, you're still going to feel the need or desire to protect them because you're used to that. You are also going to feel jealous if they speak to someone else, even though they are allowed to do that being single, because subconsciously you're thinking that by being friends you're still together.

I think years down the line, once you have lived separate lives, met different people, and dated around, there is the possibility of being friends with someone you loved deeply. However, even crossing paths with them ten years down the line, you'd probably still have a place in your heart for them if you truly were in love with them.

How would a new partner take you being friends with your ex?

Honestly, I would hate it. That is a little hypocritical coming from me because I am friends with my exes and nothing is ever going to happen between us again, but hearing someone is friends with their ex, you just are going to think, *Oh, there is unfinished business there.*

Any new partner is not going to want to be reminded of the ex partners of the person they are now in love with – especially if they text all the time or speak on the phone, or even still meet up and go for drinks. It would make anyone feel uncomfortable and it is something to consider when moving forward with someone new. If you are in love with someone and plan on spending the rest of your life with them, if something makes them feel uncomfortable, you need to think about potentially changing it.

Of course, no one ever wants to be in the breakup stage. I am single, and I still dread breakups and almost foreshadow them in future relationships because I so desperately want to avoid feeling that pain again. There are healthy ways to deal with this situation, like we've discussed, so if you do find yourself in this stage, although it feels very much like you're going to be in it forever, remember, you won't be. Each day the light at the end of the tunnel becomes that little bit brighter and closer. Just take one day at a time.

Diary Entry

I guess this is a good time to give you an update following on from my diary entry in Chapter 5, when I met up with my ex while severely hungover. Since then I have decided not to see him again. He has asked, a few times, and I debated it every single time, but there was something telling me I just shouldn't go, maybe because deep down inside I knew that I was not ready.

Although I realise this sounds contradictory, given I've just said I'm not ready, I went on a date with someone new last week, but this really did confirm my feeling. I know this because he is exactly my type — looks-wise, personality, he was everything I would want in a boy — but I just felt no spark. Then, when I woke up next to him in the morning (yes, you don't need to be a scientist to work out how the night ended), I just felt like I wanted to be on my own, despite him being an incredible guy. I met him on Hinge, which is not a shock to anyone this far into the book, but we both said on the date that we weren't looking for a relationship right now, hence why it ended the way it did. In all honesty, I feel like I needed it to end that way so I could evaluate where I was at within myself and my sexual confidence. Coming out of my relationship many months ago, I hadn't slept with anyone else because

I lost a lot of confidence and was too worried that I wasn't going to be good enough in the bedroom, which is a sad thought but one that many of us experience at some point in life. Having sex with a stranger, so I felt like I could just be free and experiment, proved to me that I do in fact have my confidence back, which was one worry ticked off my list.

I'm happy that my ex and I are friends and I hope it can remain that way for many years to come.

Chapter 8

Lessons I Have Learnt

WRITING THIS BOOK has been one big lesson for me and the last six months of my life have been truly eye-opening when it comes to the scary world of dating. If anything, this process has made me realise that I no longer want to prioritise finding someone, but to instead prioritise myself, my happiness and my dreams, so that when I am meant to meet that special person, they will enter my life when they are *meant* to, and everything will just make sense.

How you love yourself is how they will love YOU

I never realised this until I reflected upon my past situations, but it is so true: if you are happy within yourself and love yourself enough, you have the power to let someone else love you but not dictate how you are loved. Loving yourself first means they will only ever add to your life, not take from it, and you will always be strong enough to know you were okay before you received their love and you will be okay if it comes to an end.

In my first situation, I most definitely did not love myself enough, hence why I craved their attention, compliments and affection so deeply. I relied on them telling me I looked good for me to be able to go out and have a good night, to almost feel validated. When they would do something wrong, I would constantly make excuses for them instead of sticking up for myself, because I was so desperate for them not to leave. I would drop everything I was doing, even for work, if it meant I could see them for an extra hour, and I would wait up, no matter how tired I was, just in case they called me in the middle of the night. That is not loving myself, that is putting someone else's happiness before my own, and it ended in heartbreak.

It ended in heartbreak because, at the time, this person was not doing this for me in return. After leaving the situation, I focused on myself – I travelled, I worked, I figured out what made me happy – and then when I realised what I truly deserved, I entered a new relationship with a whole different mindset. And no, that relationship didn't work out either because I realised I needed longer to heal and work on my own feelings, but because I entered that relationship in a whole different mindset, knowing what I deserved and what I now expected from someone else, I attracted that, and that is exactly what I got. Loving yourself is not an easy journey; it's one that I have been on for several years and I am still nowhere near the finishing line, but everything about it is beautiful.

Whilst writing this book, Byron, who you have heard from several times, went from being in a three-year relationship to unexpectedly becoming single. This was tough, yet it is something he is now starting to realise needed to happen for him to begin his own self-love journey. These are his tips, and then I'll give you mine.

Byron's POV:

Ahh, here we go, this is the part of the book where Anna has asked me to 'wrap it up' to talk about 'what I have learnt through my experiences in love' and, if I am completely honest, I don't really know what I can say to anyone after the year I have been through. I hope when you're reading this, time will have done its job and healed me, as they say, or at least I hope I just stop believing every tarot card reader I see on TikTok.

As I am writing this, I have recently come out of my first ever serious relationship. I never really saw myself with someone; growing up I never really dated. To be honest, I never really cared to. Until obviously I somehow found myself in a situation where I fell head over heels for a boy and then suddenly almost three years had passed. I am telling myself 'all good things must come to an end' because I think that makes it easier for me to carry on with my head held high, but I never wanted it to end. Some people just suck. But here is what it taught me (I think).

1. Do not waste time worrying about someone else; if you're constantly second-guessing someone or feeling anxious about someone's actions when they are out of your control, then maybe that is your sign to leave.
2. Enjoy what you have whilst you have it. Everything is temporary. Live in the moment and appreciate those around you.
3. Don't settle out of fear of losing someone. Most of the time the idea of losing them isn't anything to do with them; they may make you feel a level of comfort and you may feel like 'the best version of yourself' whilst you are around them, but that is not them – you had that in you all along.
4. Communication is key. You must be honest with yourself and your partner if you want something to work. No matter how big or small the issue is, talk it out.
5. I am going to throw out a very gay quote from a very gay man, but it is true: 'If you

> can't love yourself, how the hell are you going to love somebody else?' It's something I didn't realise until now.

I think the last point is the most important lesson anyone can learn. Sometimes society and social media might make you feel as though it's a rite of passage to date and to have a boyfriend or girlfriend in your twenties, but let this be your reminder that you can just focus on yourself. In fact, I think that is the biggest thing I have taken away from my previous relationship. You really can't love someone else wholeheartedly if you don't love yourself wholeheartedly. Your relationship will become something that brings out your insecurities and anxieties if you are not 100 per cent comfortable with yourself, and that is what I am working on now. I want to feel completely content with who I am before I invest in someone else … I just experienced a few bumps in the road to realise that.

How did I learn to love myself?

Step 1: Recognition – Recognising that you aren't happy, or loving yourself enough, is the first step in being able to do something about it. In a lot of ways, this can be the hardest part. No one wants to admit to themselves they aren't happy, but once you do, little steps can be made to work on this. I recognised this in myself whilst speaking to someone else because I came to realise that me seeking happiness from them was only to fill the void within myself, and no one else can fill that void like you can.

Step 2: Be kind to yourself – Being kind to yourself is probably one of the hardest things you can do in this modern world where everyone lives their life on social media and constantly compares themselves to everyone they see online. Being kind to yourself isn't just about loving the body you are in, it is also about falling in love with yourself, and your soul.

Step 3: Change your self-talk – Changing the way you speak to yourself and about yourself matters more than anyone probably realises. Start by making small changes, such as instead of saying, 'My boobs aren't big enough, no one is ever going to find me attractive,' say 'I like my smaller boobs, they are what make me, me.' Positive affirmations can change the entire way you view yourself and are such an easy change to make in your everyday life.

Step 4: Allow yourself to make mistakes – Being angry at yourself for making a mistake is only going to cause continued hurt for you – no one else. Life is all about messing up and making mistakes because if everyone got it perfect all the time, it would be very boring. Mistakes are made to learn from, and like everything in life, they happen for a reason. If you make mistakes along the way, it's okay, just recognise what went wrong to ensure it doesn't happen again.

Step 5: Accepting yourself – I don't think I have hit this stage yet – I would say I am still firmly stuck in Step 4 and might be for a few more years – but loving yourself ends in, essentially, accepting yourself for who you are. I have learnt that you may never fully accept yourself, and that is also okay, but being content with the person you are and the body your soul has been placed in is a beautiful point in life to reach and one that I hope all of you reading this, if you haven't already, get to reach at some point in the future.

Forming a healthy relationship with someone else is what most people hope for, but I am currently striving for a healthy relationship with *myself*, and this is how I plan on doing so.

I surround myself with people who make me happy – As I am growing up and getting older, I have most definitely made my circle smaller, and I now only spend time with people who add something to my life or to my happiness. I used to have a lot of toxic friendships and was too scared to walk away from them out of fear of having no one, but leaving school and forming my current friendship group has made me realise I have everyone I truly need. Everyone in my life adds to it in a positive way now, and I don't feel like any of the friendships are forced or one-sided.

I enjoy being silent – This might be a very weird one for some people, but the sound of silence is bliss for me. I have become so comfortable with my own company that as much as I love seeing my friends and going out to have fun, I love a night in with my candles lit, a good dinner ready to be cooked and a new Netflix series ready to be watched. I have got quite good at being able to switch off my mind and enjoy the silence, but this took time, so don't worry if you don't get there straight away. I used to hate being on my own, silence was a scary thing for me, but slowly you learn that being okay in your own company is one of the most powerful attributes to have and no one can ever touch that.

I've started to eat better – I never realised how much my diet would affect the way I loved myself, but fuelling my body with good food and nutrients has not only made me feel physically better but has vastly improved my mood and general mental well-being. I discovered lots of new foods that I like to eat, such as salmon, prawns and avocado, and I make a conscious effort to sit down and meal plan for the weeks that I am at home. Doing this has set me in more of a routine, which I think I craved before, and has enabled me to feel better about the way I look, too. When I was sad, I would often turn to junk food or takeaways because I had no energy to want to cook or make nutritious meals, but as I have got further into building a healthy relationship with myself, I have realised that my mood is affected by what I put in my body.

I am conscious of my position – When I say this, I mean I am aware that I am surrounded by good people, live in a beautiful city and, most importantly, am healthy. Little things that I used to take for granted, like waking up and looking at huge skyscraper buildings, I now find joy in because I remember how badly I wanted that as a child. Waking up every day and being healthy, after suffering with medical anxiety for months, is something I am hugely thankful for. It's about taking every little positive win in life and being thankful for them because there was one stage in life where you craved to be where you are right now, so remaining thankful and aware is a key part of maintaining that healthy, balanced relationship with yourself.

I've started to say no – I used to be horrendous at simply using the word no because I feared disappointing people and felt like I always needed to be available to maintain friendships. Getting older and being single for a while now has made me realise that saying no is very healthy and allows you to live a balanced life and do what YOU want to do. If someone gets upset because you have said no to doing something, you must simply let it go. Ever since I have started saying no, I have felt my happiness levels grow and stress levels decrease significantly, because I'm waking up every day doing what I want to do without relying on anyone else for my happiness. Which leads me onto my next point . . .

I now rely on myself, and only myself – I am very lucky in my life to have people I can go to when I am sad or if I need help with something, but for my happiness, I rely on me. After craving validation from other people who couldn't give me that, I was forced to find my own happiness and provide that for myself, and I did that by doing all the things I mention above.

You're probably still asking, but how? You must want it so badly that you give yourself no option but to rely on *YOU*.

Final Diary Entry

I'm going to be honest here: writing the end of this diary, I am probably the most single I have been throughout this entire writing process, but I feel like it was meant to happen that way. I was scrolling through Hinge last night and some of the chat-up lines did make me giggle, such as:

'The photo of you pouring Cîroc into your mouth is how I want you to look at me.'

'What's my wife doing on this app?'

'My dad bod would fill your toned stomach like batter in a waffle iron.'

The third one absolutely sent me, because what a wild thing to say to someone. I'm going to give the second one a chance because he is beautiful, but I think the other two chat-up lines are a bit much for me. Writing this diary has been a real emotional release and a real rollercoaster of situations; one minute I am going on a date with someone and the next I am getting ghosted, but it really is all for the plot, and in my dating life, the plot is only just beginning.

ANNA X

Choosing myself

Growing up in this generation I have found it to be very rare to come across someone who isn't remotely bothered about finding a relationship. It has almost become embedded in us that we must do everything we can to find that person, and if it doesn't work out with someone, to move on to the next. This was until I had a conversation with one of my best friends, Freya. I have always known her to not go on a lot of dates, nor does she ever speak about boys, but I never really knew why until we had this conversation. I've picked out a few parts that I truly related to, to try to understand why my brain is similarly wired this way. If you feel like this too, it might help you to understand you aren't alone.

Freya: *'I never knew how to converse with men.'*

As soon as this was mentioned, it almost unlocked a part of my brain I never knew existed. It might sound so crazy – what do you mean you don't know how to converse with men? They are human. Yes, they are, but growing up with a single mother meant I barely had any interactions with adult males. As I have grown older, I have always struggled to form friendships with straight men: 90 per cent of my guy friends are gay and we might peck as a joke or say we fancy each other ten times in a day just for a laugh, but doing this with a straight man is a whole different ball game. I wouldn't just run up to one of my friends like Dev and kiss him. He'd think I was into him. I have got so comfortable within my friendship group that trying to build a connection with someone outside of the group who is straight seems a little harder for me than it would for a lot of people because, truthfully, I just don't know what to say. I am getting better at it, but if you struggle to hold friendships with the opposite sex, you are not alone. I felt instant comfort knowing Freya also felt the same.

Freya: *'I changed my outer appearance for myself, not for male validation, but I still don't feel like I want to be in a relationship.'*

This is why everything you do in life should be for you and no one else. I relate to Freya, I have tried at different points in my life to lose weight or to gain weight, or I've styled my hair differently, but ultimately, it is what is on the inside that counts. Even when I felt my best physically, I still didn't feel ready for a boyfriend because

I was not mentally ready. Of course, work on your appearance if that is what you want to do, but remember to remain in a healthy cycle with it, and not to get carried away to feel like you fit in with society.

Freya: *'Sometimes I do feel like it would be nice to have a boyfriend, but for someone to take me on and for me to take someone on I would need to be in the best mindset and be the best version of myself, but I don't think I'm there yet.'*

Being able to love another person is a beautiful thing, something that one day in the future I cannot wait to experience. I love hearing people talk about love, because everything about it sounds like everything I have ever dreamt of. But it can't be rushed or forced, it must happen when it is meant to happen. Yes, I can change my appearance, I can change how I converse with people, I could become more confident, but all of that doesn't equate to being able to love another person.

Freya: *'I'm so sick of people saying that love is all a woman is fit for . . . but I'm so lonely.'*

This is a quote that Freya told me from the film of *Little Women*, and it truly is the daily internal battle I face with myself. I wouldn't say I feel lonely all the time, but the feeling does crop up every now and then. Everyone wants to be this strong, independent, do-it-all-yourself woman – and so you should be, but it is also okay to admit that sometimes it gets lonely. I love doing things on my own and I love silence, but that also doesn't mean that a little part of me doesn't crave silence, but with another person sat loving the silence with me.

Anna: *'Being loved and loving someone isn't the same thing. I want the love to be equal on both sides.'*

I said this to Freya off the back of her telling me she had heard someone say they no longer worry about being loved. This was another internal battle I was conquering with my last relationship. I craved being loved by somebody, and I felt loved, but I did not love him in equal amounts – I physically could not. Therefore, I realised it was time to leave. I want to be able to give the same amount of love back that is given to me in a relationship, no matter how much I crave to be loved. Loving myself comes first, and then it can be equal.

Freya: *'All of TV is people in their twenties dating, so is social media, all our friends are dating, it is almost what is* *expected of us, but I know myself and I know I can't do that – I'm not comfortable with doing that.'*

And that is okay. I'm not either.

Freya: *'I have big boobs, I know I have a nice bum, but I don't dress for the male gaze, I dress for me because I want to.'*

I often get told online that I dress a certain way to attract boys, all because I have somehow grown a massive pair of boobies and enjoy wearing low-cut tops. No, I wear those outfits for me, because I think I look good. If a man compliments me that is now a bonus in my eyes, I don't need a male's opinion on my outfit to know that I look good.

Anna: *'I feel like I've reached a point now where I am so independent that I can't imagine it any other way. It's almost as though I have gone too far into my own love journey because now, I don't want anyone to change that.'*

And that is also okay. I was really thinking about this because it does worry me sometimes. Am I ever going to be able to let someone in on a deeper level or am I too scarred from the hurt I have previously experienced? Will someone sweep me off my feet and will it all make sense? I hope so, but if it doesn't, I know I am at a happy place in my life that I can continue to live at and be content. I'm protecting my own energy and will only lower those guards for someone when I get that feeling of 'you just know'.

Anna: *'My life feels peaceful again knowing I'm no longer dependent on someone else providing me with validation in order for me to be able to get on with my day.'*

Listening to this back made me tear up, because I remember how dependent I used to be on someone just to be able to wake up and enjoy my day. I completely lost my ability to be happy on my own terms and gave all the power to someone else. It was painful losing my sense of self, waking up sad every day because there was no 'good morning' text, checking my phone every ten minutes whilst I was working to see if they had messaged yet. I felt horrendous every day losing that little bit of me due to trying to love someone else, and this is what kickstarted me into making change. I no longer wake up and expect a message from anyone and I don't need to hear from anyone for me to be able to enjoy my day to the fullest. Now, I wake up excited because I know I'm not going to feel sad as soon as I pick up my phone.

Freya and Anna: *'Both of our mums are single mums, and they are both just fine.'*

I think part of the reason I feel so okay with being single now is because I see my mum single and thriving and never letting it get her down. She is so independent, she has been raising my little brother, Atticus, for the last ten years all on her own and has been the most incredible mum to me as well. My mum has taught me that in life you've got to count on yourself and no one else, because you are the only person you can ever really trust.

Anna: *'In some ways, I think the journey is the best part.'*

When I said this, I truly meant it: the journey really is the best part. Growing into having a healthy relationship with myself over the last few years has consisted of so many ups and so many downs – probably more downs than I originally hoped for, but mistakes are made to be learnt from. When reading this book, I hope you have done so with a very open mind and understood what the true meaning of it has been.

I wanted to write this book because I experienced my first heartbreak, and in every heartbreak, there is a reason – this book being mine. I will continue to date because it is something that I enjoy doing, but I no longer need it to feel like I have accomplished something in my twenties. Growing into an adult and becoming the best version of myself has been a beautiful struggle and one that I will forever be proud of. I have proved to myself that I am strong enough to enjoy the silence. I am strong enough to wake up every single day and choose myself, and I am strong enough to take the opportunity of living life on my terms. I've realised that I am no less of a person because I haven't found my person, wherever they may be, but for now, I choose me.

Acknowledgements

To the two most important women in my life, my mum Julie and nan Wendy. Thank you for showing me that being a single woman is nothing to be afraid of, and that being one has built so much strength, drive and power which has been passed down from generation to generation, and now to me. Thank you both for believing in me and sacrificing all you had in order for my dreams to come true. Now they have. I couldn't love you both any more if I tried. Us, forever and always.

To my beautiful brother Atticus. The most special, loving boy who is growing up a little too fast for his big sister's liking. Thank you for always putting a smile on my face, for calling me every day so we can eat dinner on the phone together, and hugging me that little bit tighter every time we have to say goodbye. You may only be ten as I write this, but you're the greatest gentleman I know. I love you, bubs.

To Byron, my bestest friend in the whole entire world. Life got that little bit brighter when you became part of it, from me showing up in your uni accommodation many years ago, to you showing up every day for me since. Your company is one I will never be tired of. Thank you for loving me for me, and thank you for being unapologetically you. You'll always have a little piece of my heart, and even though I'm terrified of falling in love, you're the one person it doesn't scare me with at all.

To Callum, where do I even begin. I have never met a more selfless, beautiful soul and I'm so glad our paths were meant to cross. You make me laugh till my stomach hurts and can turn a bad day into a good day just by being by my side. Thank you for walking into my life and showing me the definition of a best friend. I count myself lucky every single day, because of you.

Haz, my darling girl. From meeting through a silly boy, to now being the bestest friend a girl could ask for. You've shown me what strength is, what determination is, but most importantly, that it's okay to let yourself fall in love, and that it's not as scary as I may think. Watching you grow into a beautiful young woman has been a blessing, and I hope I'm at least half the person you are one day. Not only is this for you, but for Anne. Every time I look at you, I see her shining from within you. I love you.

Freya, my baby girl Freya. My favourite part of the day is waiting for your name to pop up on my phone to ask what we're doing for dinner. You're just one of the most loving, caring people I have ever had the pleasure of meeting, and doing life with you by my side, through the struggles, the tears, the laughs and the achievements, is one of life's biggest blessings. Thank you for opening up to me, thank you for trusting me, and thank you for being the bestest friend. I love you, baby.

Saffron, my partner in crime. The minute you walked into my bedroom when we were teenagers, I just knew you were going to be in my life forever. Growing up, doing this crazy journey of life by each other's side has been more than we could have ever asked for, and watching you achieve your goals and becoming the best version of yourself is enough to fuel me into being the best version of me. I'm grateful for everything, but especially you. I'm endlessly proud, and I love you always.

Joshua, my best friend with better hair than me, as much as it pains me to admit. You make me laugh, more than I have ever laughed before, and the excitement never gets old of you coming to stay with me, and raiding my snack drawer at 2am. Thank you for always checking in on me, for making sure I'm okay, and for cheering me on when I need it. I love you, stay slaying.

Cal, you're living proof that it doesn't matter how long you've known someone, you can feel like you've known someone a lifetime, even if it's only been a few years. Thank you for trusting me, for being my biggest cheerleader, and for cooking the most unbelievable cheese toasties when I don't have time to cook lunch. Let's keep doing life like this together, it's pretty fun.

Tanesha, my beautiful best friend from day one. You've stuck by my side as life blew me in a different direction, and have never failed to support every decision, silly or not, I've made, because that is what a best friend does. We've got each other forever, and I can't wait to explore the world with you one birthday trip at a time. Keep doing me proud, I love you unconditionally.

Dev, Doyle & Joel, the three boys who, despite life carrying us in different ways, will always be there to cheer me on. I'm proud of you all, and thankful for our friendship. I love you three, more than you'll probably ever realise.

Paige, my incredible manager. I know she will be reading this thinking, 'Anna, why are you writing me in your acknowledgements,' but Paige, you deserve it more than anyone. Working with you over the years has made this job ten times easier for me and I can't thank you enough for being such a big driving force behind my dreams all coming true. Nothing ever goes unnoticed, and I've got a lot of love for you, always.

Flossie, Sophie, Jasmine, Tia. The girlies. Having a girl group was all I ever wished for, and my wish came true. I love all of you so much, and opening our group chat to whatever chaos is occurring will be the highlight of my day even when I'm 40.

To all of my followers, some of whom have watched me grow up from a shy, little girl to the confident young woman I am now. Thank you for believing in me, sharing my life with me, and caring enough about me to want to watch whatever the hell I'm doing. This book wouldn't be possible without you – yes, you reading this right now – and I hope one day I can thank each and every one of you for changing not just my life, but my family's life too. Dreams can come true, and that's all thanks to you.

Finally, I guess I should thank my exes, and the boys I've been on dates with. I guess this book wouldn't be much without you, and each one of you has led me to the place I am now: happy.

Glossary

There are so many different terms in this book that might need a little bit of extra explaining, so I thought I would delve into them here so you can make a little more sense of them. I've also thrown in some that we haven't explored yet.

Beige Flags – These are weirdly kind of fun and maybe I am a bit strange for liking them. They are something that makes a person unique but could be deemed to be slightly annoying. An example could be when someone goes out and leaves all the lights on, or they don't ever turn the TV off. They are simple things or habits that someone has that can drive you a little crazy. I think it spices up the relationship and makes it fun, personally.

Breadcrumbing – This describes a situation when someone will show interest here and there but without any true intent of growing a real relationship. It could technically be seen as a form of manipulation as they are only doing it to keep you around in the hope you won't find someone else.

Cuffing Season – A period in the year, most commonly winter, where people get into a relationship. It's most common around the big holidays like Christmas because people want someone to go on cute dates with, but then when the summer rolls around, the relationship can become a bit rocky and sometimes break off. If I am getting into a relationship, I want it to be for the long run, not just for the cold months.

Gaslighting – In the modern-day dating world, this one is becoming a little too common for my liking. Gaslighting is a manipulation technique making someone alter their perception of a situation or understanding of an event to make it feel like they are in the wrong, when they are not. It can make the person feel like it is always their fault. Not cute at all.

Ghosting – This is where the person you are in a romantic situation with suddenly stops replying and ignores you without giving a reason. It's incredibly cruel; even if you aren't feeling it with someone, a reason should be given just for their peace of mind if nothing else.

Green Flags – these are good things that you see in the person you are dating. For example, him holding the door open for you or him not hiding his phone from you. Each person will probably have a different example of a green flag, or at least what they perceive as one, but it's all good things.

'Hey, you' – The infamous chat-up line that is going to haunt me forever. Look, if you want to subtly flirt, I am telling you this is the way to do it. I'm not saying it works every time, but it is a little more exciting than just a simple 'hello'. Try it and let me know how you get on with it.

Hook Up – A hook up can begin as just a kiss, but for some people can mean sealing the package deal. You're just having a quick kiss? You hooked up. You went back with him after a night out? Yeah, enjoy the hook up, girl.

Hinge – Or Anastasia's favourite dating app as you may now know it after reading this book. It's a dating app I have had luck on, and I think it requires slightly more effort than other apps, meaning if you're on there, you probably are looking for something a little more serious, not just a hook up.

Love Bombing – When the flattery and compliments seem rather extreme after only a few dates, you could be experiencing this. On the second date, if they are claiming you are everything they have been looking for, or are already in love with you, I'd politely decline the offer of a third date. It's a tactic they use so they automatically become the most important person in your life, which, when you think about it, is very scary.

Red Flags – Well, quite the opposite of a green flag. A red flag is a warning sign, or non-negotiable. As soon as you see one of these it is important to mention it immediately so it can get resolved, or run in the other direction, sis. A few examples would be him still messaging his ex or lying about where he is.

Situationship – Not quite a relationship, but more than a hook up. This is just the awkward, horrible stage no one ever wants to be in because it is rare you come out of this in a positive way. You end up in one of these most of the time due to lack of proper communication, so ensure to always be honest, and talk to the person you're seeing to avoid this one.

Soft Launch – Ugh, we love one of these. When you want to slowly sneak someone into your social media without making it too obvious who it is, a soft launch is for you. You post a subtle photo on your Instagram story of their hand on your leg, or a dinner table with two drinks, or even a hand on a steering wheel. Something to suggest you are with someone in more than a friendship way but aren't quite ready to post who it is yet. You can have fun with this so enjoy this stage! Every time I have done it, however, it has gone horribly wrong, so err on the side of caution.

The Ick – I can almost guarantee you have heard this phrase floating around the modern-day dating world because it is certain you're going to experience it with someone at some point. The dreaded ick is something you see someone do or a personality trait that you really don't like. People have silly icks, and half the time the ick is just an excuse to get out of the situation. You know what they say: you'll never get the ick with the right person.